Two Continents and One Island

My Long and Winding Journey from the Tropics to the Tropicana

D1392286

Abel Ndambasha

Fulton Books, Inc.
Meadville, PA

Published by Fulton Books 2021

ISBN 978-1-64952-500-0 (paperback)
ISBN 978-1-64952-501-7 (digital)

Printed in the United States of America

CONTENTS

Appendix

ACKNOWLEDGMENTS

First and foremost, I give glory, praise, and honor to Jehovah, my King, who made this book possible. He is my all in all, and without Him, I can do nothing.

Mom, I was inspired to write this book in the hope of keeping your memory alive for future generations to acknowledge that you were the catalyst that made it all possible. Even after so many years since your departure, it still feels like yesterday. How I wish you had lived long enough to enjoy the fruits of your labor manifested in the son you raised! The tears that gushed uncontrollably as I drafted the manuscript, each time I invoked your memory, were certainly not in vain. Rather they speak volumes that your legacy still lives on. This book is dedicated in its entirety to your memory.

Catherine, thank you for believing in me even in those moments when I doubted myself. You came into my life when I most needed you, and you have been a fixture by my side in my darkest hours. You gave yourself up sacrificially to see me happy. Next to God's love, yours transcends all my misgivings and indiscretions. Without you, I would not be where I am today. In the end, you inspired something beautiful out of my life.

While I always had a burning desire to tell my unique story, I would be remiss if I did not acknowledge that had it not been for my brother and good friend for life, Dr. Mwale, this book would not have materialized. Thank you, bro, for having the vision to perceive that our unique experiences across several lands would make a book project worthy of exploration. Your suggestion was the impetus that led to the culmination of this venture.

To my good friend Mwengu, whom I am proud to call a brother for life, the stories and laughter we have shared over the years, almost

5

daily, provided the stimulus that made this book a worthy response. I love you, bro, through thick and thin. When one of us is called home to glory, I cannot even begin to fathom how empty life will be.

I also wish to acknowledge my good friend Liywali, who graciously made herself available and meticulously reviewed (across the oceans) the entire manuscript in its infancy, sacrificing countless hours of personal time. In the end, it was your editing skills and valuable recommendations that led to the successful completion of the manuscript. Liywali, your selflessness and sense of duty are traits that uniquely distinguish you above the ordinary. I am grateful that we reconnected after almost forty years. I will remain indebted to you for the rest of my mortal life. Merci, mon amie.

To the Garcia and Delgado families, to Raquel, thank you for putting yourselves at God's disposal, as human angels in the service of the Master Weaver. I pray that God, who is rich in mercy, will find a way to repay your kindness more than I could ever possibly do.

To my daughters (nieces), and grandbaby Lusayo, Penelope, Linga, and Salome, thank you for the joy that seeing you blossom into beautiful and responsible young women brings to my life. I have no doubt that the good Lord has a unique calling for each one of you. Continue to stir and pursue the talents that God has blessed you with. I love you always.

To my nephews Abel, Hope, and Destiny, I pray that you will grow to understand and appreciate that the secret to success consists of putting God above all else.

PREFACE

In the middle of writing this book, I was asked a poignant question by a colleague I ran into at a supermarket. She wanted to know why I would choose to write a book about my life in the absence of name recognition or an established fan base. I do not believe I gave her a satisfactory answer, but I mumbled my response to the effect that it will be worth it even if it resonates with only one individual across the entire globe. This memoir is certainly not a story about my rise from poverty to riches; neither is it a story about self-aggrandizement. It is simply a story of my unique life's journey, a story of hope and destiny, courage, and perseverance. It is intended to demonstrate God's goodness and favor at every turn. I did not write this book in pursuit of personal glory or fame, let alone the treasures the world has to offer. I was simply motivated by the desire to be an instrument in the service of my Master, adding my voice to the chorus.

First and foremost, I wrote this book to acknowledge and honor my Maker. It is my sincere belief that the Lord orchestrated my life in His own fashion and directed every footstep through the various phases of my life. As a boy growing up in Zambia, little did I know what lay ahead, but even at that tender age, I had a burning desire to have a closer relationship with my Maker. When I surrendered my life to Him as a young lad, I presumed that everything would be smooth sailing from then onward. I had no expectations of a bumpy ride ahead of me. As someone once said, it is a fearful thing to fall in the hands of a living God in the context that it is no longer just about me, that it is about His overarching will and His way. The process of taking us to new heights is one that I have observed to be full of ups and downs because as humans, we are inclined to put up resistance when we don't see immediate results or obtain instant gratification. Certainly, God's way of dealing with us may include taking us to places not conducive to our personal comfort, but He does what it takes to ultimately mold us more to His liking. I believe this to be my experience over the years. I had no idea that I would end up where I am today, in my wildest dreams. However, the Lord who works in mysterious ways, His wonders to perform, had it all figured out. Whenever I reached the crossroads of life and did not know where to turn, His grace was always sufficient for my needs. Did I make the wrong decisions sometimes? You bet, but even when I did, His correction was always measured and focused me on the bigger picture, ensuring that I grasped essential lessons I could draw upon for the future.

My second motivation for writing this book was to show that there are human angels, whom God uses to execute His plan in our favor. Throughout my journey, there have been numerous examples of human angels that God brought into my life just at the right time to meet my specific needs. The Garcia and Delgado families are just two examples. The selflessness and kindness they showed to a total stranger such as me was unbelievable. Yet in my heart of hearts, I knew that it was God who prepared them uniquely to cater to my needs.

At a deeper level, there were some things that I had kept to myself for a long time. By bringing them out in the open through this channel, I believe this to be a step in the right direction in terms of inner healing and closure, even as I acknowledge God's capacity for forgiveness. There is no denying that over the course of my life, I have done certain things that I should not have done, as I knew better. It is, I believe, a call to take heed, a warning to all as reflected in the thought "Let him who thinks he stands, take heed lest he falls." I fell so many times, but the good news is that we have an advocate within the Godhead, who intercedes for us with sighs too deep for words. He takes pleasure in restoring us to our former glory, no matter how big the fall might seem.

I also wanted to honor the memory of my mother through this medium. The saying that "Behind a successful man, there is always a woman" certainly is in line with one's mother by implication. My mother was a positive influence in my life. She was my role model growing up. She knew how to touch the right buttons to keep me motivated from a very young age. First, she instilled the fear of God in me and then taught me the value of hard work. She then followed through with imparting knowledge that allowed me to stay focused on the goal, avoiding distractions. While she was not schooled in leadership curriculum, she always insisted on *not* being a follower but in leading by example and being the first to take the initiative or dissenting view in the face of rampant cowardice.

In the end, yes, I was motivated by the thought that someone somewhere may be going through tumultuous times and wondering if there is help out there. My resounding answer is that there is help without a doubt. We can trust God for whatever challenges life may bring our way, from the complex issues to the mundane. If my experience can point someone to their Maker, that will be an outcome far greater than the entire world can possibly offer. God does care about our lives, as perennial as they might seem—here today and gone tomorrow. While we will never understand how God works in terms of the whys and hows, He takes pleasure in addressing our specific needs. In His wisdom, He knows what is best for every individual. We have all been uniquely endowed to fulfill different roles for the glory of His name. For this very reason, every life is unique, and there is not a one-size-fits-all solution. If we can only trust and wait upon Him, His promise is that we will not wait in vain; that is the trust we certainly need to imbibe if God be for us. My hope and prayer for everyone who reads this book is that they will, by God's grace, endeavor to establish a deeper relationship with the Creator Himself and seek to walk in His ways no matter the cost. So help us God...

Pseudonyms are used throughout the book to disguise the identity of some of the characters.

BACKGROUND

In the tropics of Central Africa lies a landlocked expanse: God's country, a land fashioned with and blessed by God's good, gracious hand, with rich mineral deposits and unrivaled natural beauty, interspersed with unique flora and fauna, not to mention the simplicity and hospitality of its people. A host of curious travelers from around the globe flock to its borders year after year, if only to catch a glimpse of the great Zambezi River, the scenic Lake Bangweulu, and of course, one of the seven wonders of the natural world—the mighty Victoria Falls. For whatever reason beyond my paygrade, it pleased Providence to designate Zambia as the land of my birth and upbringing.

I was born the second child, and grew up in a family of four siblings. Salient childhood memories take me back to that corner house on the east end of Lufwanyama Street in the small town of Kalulushi on the Copperbelt Province. This was the house I grew up in, in the mid-1960s. The corner location on our street translated into the unusual advantage of having an extended backyard, which my mother conveniently put to good use. She grew corn (maize), beans, and other seasonal crops to supplement our livelihood. We had, in addition, several mango trees and later an avocado tree, which yours truly planted and nurtured till fruition. My father, like most working men at the time, worked in the copper mining industry, which was by most accounts the lifeblood of the Zambian economy.

Zambia was then a young nation. Having attained political independence from Great Britain in October 1964, the country was desperate to transfer ownership of the economy from the colonial masters' control into indigenous hands. As one of the founders of national independence predicted, and rightly so, "colonialists would be back over time, disguised as investors" to continue their quest to rape and plunder the country of its resources in complicity with our inept public officials.

My parents, like most of our neighbors, had migrated from their home village to the booming towns on the Copperbelt in search of economic opportunities, which were plentiful at the time. Most jobs in the mining industry did not require much skill or dexterity; manual labor skills were the average yardstick used to assess employ-ability. Those who could speak the little English acquired in grade school fared even better in the face of ample work opportunities.

The migration of our parents to the thriving towns on the Copperbelt, and other major urban centers, represented a major transformation in the demographics of Zambian and African society at large. Those of us born in the pre-independence era (starting in the mid-1950s) represented the first generation of Africans born and raised outside the confines of a village establishment associated with respective tribal groups. While our parents did their best to inculcate the language and customs that had been passed on to them by their forebears, we were a different breed—a generation faced with unique opportunities to shape the future of a young nation. Our calling and responsibility were to assimilate the white man's education to the highest degree possible and use it to transport our society into the postmodern era. Little did we know that this was a daunting task that we were completely unprepared to embrace as torchbearers.

Consciously or subconsciously, we focused on creating our own identity, separate from that of our parents' world. We questioned traditional values, demanded explanations for the status quo, and challenged authority on an array of issues, even to the point of embracing illicit drugs. We questioned the inferior role of women in society, the role of the white man's religion in African society, and how Christianity was used as a tool to colonize our minds.

We grew up speaking the local language, known as Bemba. Understandably, in a society comprised of diverse cultural back-grounds, a common language denominator was imperative. Not only was Bemba a vehicle that bonded our communication experience, but it was also the medium that set us apart from our parents' world and allowed us to forge our unique identity in a rapidly evolving society. As we started to learn English in primary school, we became uniquely positioned to interact with the Western world and thus exposed our blank slates to the moldings of Western cultural influences through music and other vices (which I will address in a later chapter).

Two Continents and One Island is the story of my life's journey and experiences lived on two continents and an island—namely Africa, North America, and the Caribbean island of Cuba. I was born and raised in Zambia, attended postsecondary school in Cuba, and thereafter, migrated to the US, where I have spent the bulk of my professional life and currently reside. While my story may not be characterized as extraordinary by many, it is certainly one of hope, replete with ups and downs, but more importantly, is a demonstration of God's faithfulness at every turn. My story begins in the all-too-familiar neighborhood that forged my way of thinking and prepared me for the *great unknown*, which we commonly refer to as life.

PART I

First Continent

CHAPTER I
The Neighborhood

The neighborhood around Lufwanyama Street where I spent my vulnerable years growing up is what shaped me to be the man I am today. To put things in context, we were poor by every measurable standard, and so was every family around us. Our families lived from paycheck to paycheck, occasionally stretching the budget by borrowing from local sharks at high interest rates, which created a cycle of dependency for most families. I must acknowledge from the onset that as poor as our parents were, they did their best to sacrifice for us, the children.

Not only did my parents raise four siblings, but they also took on the additional responsibility of caring for two of my cousins, whose parents were not in a position to care for them for reasons beyond my understanding at the time. Our cousins were older than us, and therefore we looked up to them as older siblings for guidance and protection. In addition to the cousins who permanently resided with us, there were other relatives from the village who showed up occasionally, mostly without prior notice. My poor mom had such a big and welcoming heart that she simply made room for everyone. My mom, like most married women in the neighborhood, did not have a paid day job. She was totally devoted to house-chores and raising the family. I observed at a very early age that this arrangement was the cause of much abuse for the women at the hands of their husbands.

Despite living in modest housing consisting of just two bedrooms, my mom found a way to accommodate everyone. Sleeping arrangements were such that my parents occupied the main bedroom, the boys shared the other bedroom, and the girls used the living room as their bedroom. The small kitchen was occasionally converted to a bedroom at night, depending on how many relatives were visiting at any given time. With only one bathroom to share in the entire household, it is anybody's guess how many near or actual bathroom misses occurred. What made it worse was that the toilet and washing areas were sub-units within the same room, and therefore if one was taking a shower, the rest of the family had no access to the toilet facilities. Did I mention we lived in a corner house with a big backyard and no backdoor neighbors? The backyard was a blessing for that reason and was put to good use despite continued protests from my parents. One other inconvenience about the house we occupied was that there was no direct access to the bathroom from the living areas. To get to the bathroom at night, one had to first exit through the main entrance in the kitchen. If it was raining at night, one had to be creative in answering the call of nature. If someone was in the kitchen sleeping, one's options were rather limited; you were better off peeing in bed and dealing with the ridicule the following morning than risking exposing yourself to the elements, or whatever creatures roamed the night. With the recognition that there were many families whose conditions were worse than ours, we counted our blessings.

Sharing the same bed with my two brothers was unavoidable. Unfortunately, I had a chronic bed wetting problem which I carried almost into the teenage years. This translated into many sleepless nights for the three of us. Every morning our mom would daringly walk into the bedroom to look for signs of wetness. The results were always the same. At one point, when our bedroom was infested with lice, my mom got so desperate that she began to ask for advice from well-meaning friends and neighbors about how to curb this behavior in her son. All kinds of suggestions were offered, verging at best on superstition and at worst, ignorance. One that caught my attention that I still recall to this day was placing a frog (*Chula wa mainsa*, in Bemba) near my tender penis. The thought was that if the frog felt any wetness, it would bite, waking me up instantly. There were those who claimed to confirm positive results through this attempt.

Somehow, my mom was not too keen on carrying this or any other proposal to fruition. This idea was probably the least awkward out of the many suggestions offered.

To say that every family in the neighborhood was dysfunctional would be an understatement. At a very young age, I discovered that men were at the apex of the social pyramid in African society by tradition. Women were expected to be submissive to their husbands, regardless of how reprehensible the men's behavior might seem. Failure to submit often resulted in very severe consequences for the poor, defenseless women. Children, on the other hand, were expected to be seen but not heard in the presence of adults.

Being the breadwinners of the family unit gave men a powerful edge to treat women like objects. It may well be that this behavior was partly rooted in the *lobola* (bride price) tradition, whereby a man was expected to pay a price to have permission to take away his bride. Beating one's wife was a common occurrence; there were only a handful of men in the neighborhood whom I recall did not beat their wife, which in some distorted fashion was treated like a sport. Interestingly, when I was in secondary school, I recall reading an article published in the local newspaper recounting the results of a survey asking women their opinions on the practice of wife beating. Sadly, the majority of the women interviewed were of the opinion that they actually welcomed this practice because it showed that the men cared for them and were simply motivated by the desire to correct bad behavior on their part. The truth is that women's choices were very limited, even if they wanted to stand up to such objectionable behavior. Often, they had nowhere to go if they chose to walk away from an abusive marriage.

My childhood innocence was however, routinely punctuated by undesirable exposure to violence. Ponder the following scenario, if you will: You wake up one morning on what promises to be a beautiful sunshine day only to see out of nowhere your father chasing your mom as the rooster does to the hen. Eventually, he catches up with her and slaps her so hard that she falls to the ground, pleading for mercy. Apparently, he is not done yet. He traps her between his legs and continues to slap her without restraint. As a kid, you can only watch and cry, probably growing up to hate your father for inflicting pain on a delicate and defenseless soul. The other men in the neighborhood do not think it is their business to intervene because they likely will be doing the same to their wives subsequently.

Or consider another scenario: Your dad comes home drunk and finds that there is no food for him. He locks the bedroom door and proceeds to make an example of your mother with no one to interfere. The following day, she wakes up and does her best to put food on the table for the "master."

That "master" was my dad—frequently abusive and victim to the overconsumption of alcohol. Seeing him walking home from the beer gardens, it was hard for me to understand why he drank so much and made such a fool of himself. I don't believe it was because he had the disposable income to spare; I could only surmise that beer was for him an escape from the pressures of family responsibilities he might have been trying to adjust to. On one occasion, having left home to drink with his buddies, he did not return home for the entire weekend. My desperate mother was beside herself, searching all over for him, including the mortuary. When he finally showed up, his only explanation was that his friends had persuaded him to go drinking in another town. My poor mom had no courage to ask any further questions, knowing that the tables would be turned against her if she proceeded with that line of inquiry. I could only shake my head in disbelief, but this was the man that brought me into the world.

As flawed as he was, he loved me and wanted me to grow up and become successful in life. Even at the tender age of five or six, I had no doubt in my mind that his behavior was beyond reprehensible, and I could not reconcile my mixed emotions toward him. These are the kind of experiences I was exposed to in my home growing up as a kid.

The neighborhood I grew up in was called Section Six. The ranking represented position and paygrade at work. Our parents in Section Six were predominantly blue-collar workers in the mining industry. Segregation by rank and level of education was a structural reality, and to this end, our parents would constantly remind us that if we wanted to live on the other side of town, education was the only bridge to success. That was probably the best lesson I ever picked up from my father. My determination to succeed was more than palpable from a very young age. Whatever it took, in so much as it depended on me, failure was not an option I was willing to embrace.

Parallel to Lufwanyama Street was Matanda Street. Directly opposite us, with no fence in between, lived another family with kids in our age group. My brothers and I cultivated great friendships with them. While the man next door drank just like my father did, he appeared more responsible. He, too, had his family issues to contend with. He would come home and verbally abuse his wife in the presence of his kids, occasionally beating her. He eventually ended up divorcing his wife. Then he went to his home village and brought back another "trophy" or, better still, a "subservient wife." Changing one woman for another was that easy. Alimony or other forms of spousal support were totally unheard of.

At the second house along Matanda Street lived a deeply religious man with his family. He was an elder in the local church we attended. The outstanding characteristic about this family was that the head of the household was married to two women and lived with both in a two-bedroom house like ours. Children around our ages were reared in this household too. As soon as they moved into the neighborhood, it didn't take long for us to embrace them as friends. All things considered, they were quite a happy family except for the rare occasions when the women engaged in physical fights. The children would also take sides with their mothers, making it look like a civil war within a family. Each time the women fought, the man would politely step in, remove the infants from their backs, and simply walk away, letting them duel it out. Fortunately, other responsible women like my mother would intervene and bring order to the chaos. What I found commendable about this man was that I never saw him beat any of his wives. He was soft-spoken and instead engaged in teaching his family biblical principles. While his practice of polygamy is questionable, it is worth mentioning that there was another family in another neighborhood not too far from ours where the man was married to two sisters. This was a common custom among a certain group from the northern part of the country, where a man would be rewarded with a second "prize" (if you will) for good behavior.

Directly opposite the previous house on Lufwanyama Street lived a family of ten, including the parents. Their house was a hive of activity in the neighborhood, especially around the Christmas holiday season. They owned a record player and had all kinds of vinyl records encompassing African and Western themes popular at the time. They were an outgoing family, associating with almost everyone in the neighborhood and beyond. The man of the house was a medicine man practicing traditional methods of diagnosis and healing. Somewhere in their house, they kept a fetish they named Kasongo, through which the man could tell who might have been responsible for a bewitching. In this household, it was the wife who wore the pants. She was the one that would slap the husband into submission whenever she thought he was out of line, sending a clear message of hope to the other women that violence against women was surmountable. Both the man and wife in this household drank excessively; as a matter of fact, the wife was in the business of brewing and selling a homemade beer, which attracted quite a few invited and uninvited guests to their house. While she put the supplemental income to the benefit of the family, it was not long before the kids were introduced to the local brew at a young age.

A man who owned a local bottle store lived along the same street. It was rumored that he had fought in the independence war alongside the first Zambian president, Dr. Kenneth Kaunda. To the best of my recollection, he was the only one on the street who owned a television set in the mid-1960s. Most of us kids would do our best to secure a spot in their backyard to be able to watch TV shows like *Batman* through their living room window or through the door, if they were kind enough to leave it open. Whenever Muhammad Ali's boxing fights were broadcast live, theirs was the venue and hive of activity that attracted the entire neighborhood.

Another house of interest along Lufwanyama Street was that of a forward-thinking man, an entrepreneur by all measurable standards, who was truly a role model. The man raised pigeons in his backyard to supplement the family income. He raised two very beautiful daughters, one of whom I had a crush on. Almost every weekend, he would organize his colleagues to play games of chance, such as cards, for financial gain. Once, I heard of a player who lost all his money and decided to bet his wife with the understanding that if he lost, the winner could have her. As expected, he lost, but we were not privy to the details of how the issue was resolved. It was rumored that the poor woman was seen leaving the house of the "winner" early one morning.

Further along the same street lived a witch doctor. He had consultations almost every week on an array of issues. There were those who wanted to know why a family member was sick or why they were passed over for promotion or how to get ahead of everyone else. The rituals always began with singing and chanting. The man had a brigade of volunteer male and female singers and enchanters that were truly dedicated to the cause. At an opportune time, the man would direct his subordinates to follow him to the alleged culprit's house, where they would start digging for the evidence, such as a mixture of herbs buried at the front entrance to the house. It did not matter if the homeowner was available. Witch doctors like him were revered and feared.

The households I just described are intended to convey the quality of the men who were entrusted with the responsibility of fostering our growth and success in society. The one common denominator about these men was that they were all flawed—addicted to the overconsumption of alcohol, abusive to women, and downright dysfunctional fathers. Nevertheless, we held them in high esteem on the principle of respect for those who gave us life. The truth is we had no other choice. How could a young man stand up to his father and ask him to try to live his life differently? However, the scars they left on our tender psyches would have lifelong repercussions, were it not for the Grace of God. In the eyes of a kid, it does not take long to forget the wrongs your dad committed the previous day.

While the issues of poverty in Africa are well-known and documented, it was odd that I never saw homeless people living under bridges. The concept of the extended family support system in the African context allowed us to provide a support structure for the needy. Growing up, we never thought of ourselves as poor, probably because we did not see too many rich people around us. We were not exposed to excesses such as are common today in the western world. We had enough to eat, clothes to wear, a roof over our heads, and were certainly blessed with friends to play with at any time. We knew all our neighbors within a radius of about a square mile. Each time that a new family would move in, they would be embraced by the community almost instantaneously.

The game of soccer was a major pastime for us growing up. This was the era of the great Brazilian Pele, whose accomplishments in the world of soccer will probably live on forever. We organized ourselves largely based on the neighborhoods we lived in and competed with other kids. There were no referees; all arbitrations were adjudicated by negotiation and consensus between the captains of the opposing teams. Unfortunately, this resulted in unwanted fights too often. There was simply no time limit on a game, but we would agree upfront say for instance, on a score of five, we would change sides and end the game on a score of ten. Games like that would last for what seemed an eternity. If the lunch hour fell in between the game time slot, no one even thought about running home to catch a bite; soccer was far too important to miss. Our satisfaction was derived from beating and taunting the opposing team before taking home the prize, which consisted of a small amount of money that the two teams would put up before the game. Most of us kids got allowances from our dads, say about twenty cents every month. These were the monies we would put up as a team to compete against another. If you did not contribute money, it meant you could not participate. There were instances when we would steal from our parents, just to make sure we would be able to play. Unfortunately, at the end of the day, when the game was over, our parents would be waiting for us—as the Cubans would commonly say, "*Como cosa buena* [as a good thing]." That meant a good beating and no dinner. However, that was a small price to pay for the love of soccer.

If we were not playing soccer, we would be out in the woods, gathering wild fruit, such as *intungulu*, *amakole* (snot apple), *inchenja*, *amasuku* (wild loquat), and *infungo*. These were seasonal fruits, mostly in bloom around the summer months. We usually had to travel more than 10 miles from the outskirts of town to be able to find what we were looking for. Most of these forests were so dense, but the sheer strength in numbers encouraged us to go even further. Occasionally, we would run into snakes and do our best to kill them immediately. At the end of a long day, we would go home and feast on our bounty with such arrogance, laughing in the face of the kids who had failed to join us on the trip.

Other activities of interest included making small models of cars using wire and playing a game we called *sojo*. To start with the latter, sojo involved sliding a round piece of metal (fabricated through casting) into a hole of about two to three inches in diameter from a distance of, say, fifty feet. The trick was in the ability to produce a metallic cast, such that the contact surface would slide with minimum friction against the concrete floor. For that, we developed and honed the art of producing castings to an almost professional level, merely using rudimentary tools we would find at a community landfill (*malabo*) and adapt to suit our needs. We played the game of sojo for buttons. These were acquired through whatever means were necessary, starting with plucking them off our own clothes and later through other dubious schemes, including stealing clothes just to have the buttons. I am not even sure what we did with the buttons other than merely sustain bragging rights.

Making wire cars was another pastime for us. The process would begin with a trip to the local landfill, which was several miles on the outskirts of town. The landfill was rich in a wide array of "memorabilia" (or so we thought). Despite multiple hazardous warning signs posted around the periphery of the site, we always found a way to break barriers to be able to get in. The stench from the landfill was strong, but our goal was to reach fresh "gold." God knows what chemicals we were exposed to in this venture. Surprisingly, no one and nothing could stop us. We knew the days of the week when deliveries from the mines were due. All we were looking for were the wires and cables discarded from several operations in the mining process. Upon our return, we would start modeling our individual cars, beginning with the base frame. Assembling a wire car took about one or two days depending on the size of the model and being able to complete a toy car that could move was such a thrilling experience for us. Little did I know that there was a "small" engineer in me, even without formally having to go through the theory of linkages and mechanisms. While my wire cars were not the best in appearance compared to those of my peers, they were the most robust.

If we were not out in the woods, playing soccer or making wire cars, we found other outlets for channeling our excess energy. Boxing was one such outlet. We would break up in pairs and beat each other, sometimes even to the point of bleeding. Often, fights were not considered complete until "silver" (blood) was observed on one of the opponents. We protected our turf from intruders. Any boy venturing into our neighborhood had to have a genuine reason for doing so, as there was a common understanding that loitering in a neighborhood you were not part of was a misdemeanor in the eyes of community justice.

Our scope of misplaced interests and values in childhood included killing *blue mutwe* (blue head) lizards and dogfighting. Several of the kids in our neighborhood had dogs, which we would engage to fight each other even if the dogs showed no appetite for it. Occasionally, we would venture out into other neighborhoods looking for other dogs which could fight those from our neighborhood. If we could not find any suitable opponents, we would look for cats and turn our dogs loose on them. It was then that I learned to give credence to the expression that cats had nine lives. We were just kids who did not know any better in terms of animal cruelty.

Fig 1: Yours truly at the age of 3.5 years (maybe) without a pair of shoes on the right with his two brothers.

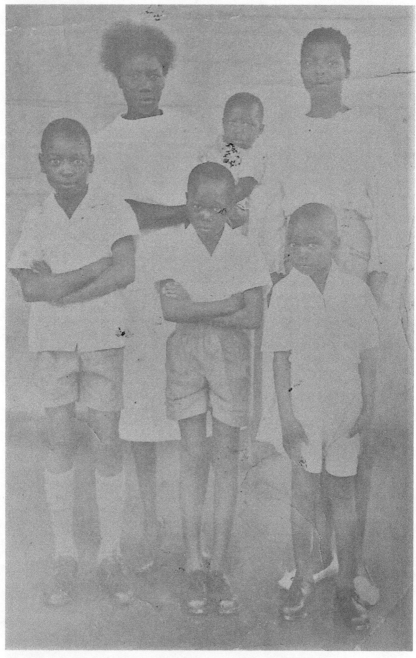

Fig 2: Yours truly at the age of 5 or 6 years (in the middle) with mom, siblings and a cousin

CHAPTER 2
The Community

The town I grew up in was considered fairly small. I would estimate the population to have been around forty to fifty thousand people. As previously mentioned, the economy of the town was largely dependent on the mining industry. The residents that did not work in the mining industry either worked for the city municipality, central government, or other private companies, such as banks. There was also a niche segment of the population that was self-employed, running small scale informal businesses, such as selling local produce at the market, or managing established grocery stores.

The city infrastructure included basic amenities, such as electricity and running water. The main roads running through the city were tarred for the most part; the other roads, although paved, were dusty and often vulnerable to weather elements such as rain. There were two sections to the city: the blue and white-collar sections. All the expatriates (mostly from Britain) lived in the white-collar section. There was also an upper class of indigenous Zambians who had made it to the top. They too lived in the white-collar section. Living in the white-collar section afforded one privileged access to all sorts of luxury amenities, like the best grocery stores, a public swimming pool, tennis courts, a golf course, and others.

If you had not made it to the ranks of the upper class, you lived in the blue-collar section. The downtown center of the blue-collar section was always a hive of activity, especially at the end of the month when the miners got their pay. This is where most of the grocery stores and pubs were located. It was also the main bus terminal to the major surrounding towns. Next to the town center was a soccer stadium, which was also the venue for other community celebrations, such as Independence Day (October 24). When the blue-collar workers got their pay at the end of the month, most of them congregated at the pubs, where there was always music playing from the jukeboxes. As *mishanga* (cigarette) and chewing gum sellers, we were all too active during the month end, hoping to cash in on the influx of disposable income. We were merely dispensable employees working for the older boys who were the real sharks of the trade.

There was always a variety of African beats playing, especially Lingala music from the Congo. The month-end was also the period of much stress for most families; there were men who got their paychecks and headed straight to the taverns. By nightfall, the men would be totally drunk and broke. Most of the men we knew growing up exhibited this kind of behavior to the point that it became the norm. There was a billboard campaign by the government attempting to discourage this rampant behavior.

What I found intriguing was that in the blue-collar section of town, there was a deliberate effort to segregate workers by rank through housing. It was extremely disconcerting to note that a family of ten could live in a single-bedroom house solely because the breadwinner was relegated to an inferior position. Unfortunately, family planning was not an option most Zambian men were willing to embrace, let alone discuss. They believed in having as many children as a man could be blessed with.

In our section of the town, there were hardly any community amenities. To be able to use the public swimming pool, we had to walk at least ten miles to reach the other side of town. Even when we did so, we could not afford to pay the entrance fee, and so our only option was to climb the trees around the swimming pool and watch from a distance while white expatriates and upper-class Zambian families enjoyed the pool. Prior to independence, the pool was exclusively for white people. Watching from up in the trees, I always wondered what it would feel like to be able to swim like I saw the other kids do. It wasn't long before the golden opportunity presented itself. Our older cousin, whom we grew up with, got a job working at the bank, and when he got paid, he gave my brothers and me enough money to pay the entrance fee. The only underwear I had at the time was good enough to be used as a swimming costume. I could not sleep the night before the day we were supposed to go to the pool; I was just so excited that for the first time, I was going to be in that clear blue water even though I had to restrict myself only to the baby section. Later that day, as I was walking past the deep-end section, one of the kids pushed me toward the water, thinking that I could swim. I almost drowned, but this turned out to be a blessing in disguise. I struggled to stay afloat; several times I was submerged, but I still managed to raise my head above the water. For some strange reason, I did not scream for help. I just kept on trying to keep my hands in motion, and the more I did, the more my head stayed above the water. By some miracle, I found myself at the edge of the pool, holding on to the supports. I had involuntarily grasped what the principle of buoyancy was all about; this was baptism by immersion. I had learned to swim by instinct on the very first day I was exposed to the pool. More importantly, I learned a valuable lesson that day: to every problem life throws at one, there is always a solution.

There were four primary schools in the city. At the age of five approaching six, my mom took me to be enrolled. To determine if I was old enough, they asked me to wrap my right arm over my head and touch my left ear. Unfortunately, my arm was not long enough. According to the school administrator, I was not ready to start school yet. She advised my mom to show up the following year. All I could do was cry all the way home. The thought of having to wait another year looked like a lifetime, especially since most of the kids I used to play with were accepted. I went back to the mundane routines I was accustomed to, but occasionally, I would bug my mom about when I was going to start school. It wasn't long before the year was over. The night before D-day, I could not sleep; I was totally consumed by anxiety.

To cut a long story short, this time I was successfully enrolled. To my delight, another primary school was under construction, which was even closer to where we used to live. We were going to be the first intake of grade 1 students privileged to walk the halls of a freshly minted primary school. Until construction was completed, we remained at the other school, for approximately six months. I still remember my first-grade teacher. He was a no-nonsense man, a strict disciplinarian who tolerated no mischief. We all respected him out of fear. In those days, teachers (supported by parents) believed in the "spare the rod and spoil the child" principle. Teachers had the liberty and discretion to punish a student as they saw fit, with the full support of parents and the community at large. One day at break time, I recall slapping a girl whom I thought was being rude to me. When she threatened to report me to the teacher, I begged her not to do it. She sensed that the consequences for me were probably going to be worse than what she had endured with me. She gave in and became my very good friend.

To say that the teacher abused us verbally and physically when we did not meet his expectations would be an understatement. I reckoned that the prevailing philosophy in child-rearing at the time was that children like us (raised in the compounds) were little devils. The only way to exorcise the demons out of their little souls was to bring them to the point of subjugation using proven instruments like the rod. Later, when I was in the fourth or fifth grade, we had another teacher who not only was an imposing disciplinarian but also sometimes showed up to class drunk. One day, one of the girls who had made it a habit to skip school regularly decided to show up. When she answered present during the daily roll call, he asked her to wait in the corner of the classroom indefinitely. As soon as he was done, he took off his belt and rolled up his sleeves. He held the loose ends of her dress with his left hand and started to beat her buttocks mercilessly. At one point, he raised her dress unintentionally to the extent that her tender vagina was left exposed for the entire class to behold. Incidentally, she was not wearing underwear, probably because her parents could not afford them for her. There were gasps from the girls in the class and jeers from the boys. He paused for a moment, commanded the class to be quiet, and proceeded with the disciplinary session. When he had completed his business, he let her loose and turned to warn the class that he was not going to hesitate to make an example of anyone who wanted to skip school. The point was well taken, as there was complete silence in the classroom. It was not long before the poor girl made the inevitable decision to drop out of school rather than face the humiliation of that experience.

On another occasion, probably in sixth grade, several boys were caught smoking marijuana in the bathroom. Classes were interrupted; a notification went out to have all the students gather at the assembly area. A table was brought and placed in the center of a U-shaped assembly area. One by one, the culprits were asked to lie down on the table, face down. Volunteers were asked to hold their limbs firmly while the teacher with the whip proceeded to execute the corporal punishment.

When the first lash was meted, the entire school shouted in unison: "One!"

On the second lash, shouts of "Two!" went out.

The cheering went on all the way until the count of twelve lashes for each of the culprits. The end of the ceremony was followed up by the usual pep talk. Such was the sense of discipline that was instilled in us growing up. Whether or not we agreed with the methods used, we had no option of voicing our opinion. We were expected to respect our teachers and follow their instructions if we wanted to be successful in life.

Aside from teachers that demanded respect, there were also bullies to be reckoned with. My nightmare was a bully by the name of Katie, a girl who fought like a man and commanded respect from every pupil. One day, sitting in the row next to hers in class, she wanted to see my answers to a test, and without much thought, I refused. She gave me that stern look and followed through with the warning: "I will see you after class." For the rest of the day, I could not focus. I felt like wanting to pee in my pants. When the final bell rang, I was the first at the door and took off like a bullet, but she ferociously came after me. Realizing that I could not outrun her, I took refuge in one of the stalls in the boys' toilet room, panting like a dog, as she paced back and forth at the entrance, taunting me to come out if I considered myself a man. After what felt like an eternity, she gave up and walked away with the warning that my days were numbered. I had escaped the jaws of an angry lioness.

After we transitioned into the new school, I made friends with a boy who used to live in the white-collar community; his name was Joe. We used to refer to their homes as *ama yadi* (plots of land) possibly because they had big yards. I do not quite recall how our friendship started since kids from the upper class considered us kids from the "locations" (compounds) as steerage. I was a good student, almost always at top of the class, and so was he, but I was just a notch above him. It was not long before he invited me to his home. It turned out that he was living with his brother, who was one of the first few Zambians who were offered scholarships to study in Europe shortly after we attained political independence. Upon his return from Europe, he brought home a trophy in the form of a white woman for a wife. That was a peculiarity at the time. Unfortunately, my friend recounted, their marriage did not last. She just could not fit into our society. When I heard this story, I made an innocent comment to the effect that perhaps one day I, too, would marry a white woman.

I invited my friend to our humble home. He was not judgmental compared to other *ma yadi* kids but embraced me as a friend despite our differences in "zip codes." We really clicked, given that we had very similar interests, the paramount of which was that we were both bookworms. The public library in my neighborhood was our favorite hideout, a refuge from the distractions we were too often exposed to. It was there that we developed and cultivated our love for reading.

Perhaps it was my deep-seated love for reading that led to development of a sleep-walking disorder. On more than one occasion, I was found at the doorsteps of the public library well past midnight by the night watchman during his routine vigilance of municipal properties. Fortunately, the man knew our family, and each time he found me, he would courteously walk me home about a mile away and present me to extremely disturbed parents. This habit was a source of real concern by my mom as she hardly slept, listening to hints of me leaving the house every night. Given all my issues in childhood, expectations of me succeeding in life were dismal at best. It was only my mom who harbored high expectations of me.

In third or fourth grade, Joe introduced me to the idea of writing a book, following in the footsteps of his older brother, who had published a book previously. I thought the idea was fascinating. We started to write a collection of short stories. When we brought the manuscript to the attention of our teacher, he could not hide his amazement, but he encouraged us to stay on course.

Not only was Joe smart, but he was also outgoing, coupled with a great sense of humor. These qualities made him very popular in school. Fast forward several decades later, I was not surprised in the least when I heard that he had risen to a cabinet position in the government and ably represented our country in the diplomatic corps. I was popular only because I was top of the class most of the time, but I was not outgoing. There were those who thought I was somewhat goofy. My teacher and role model, Mr. Mamunye, gave me the nickname *Smiler* after a popular cartoon character as it was just in my nature to smile at everything life threw at me. My closest companions understood that my youthful joy was as wide as my smile.

Not long afterward, I met another pupil in the same school and grade but different class designation. His name was Pat. This kid was also top of his class. The convenience that he lived closer to my home made it easier for us to socialize more frequently. After visiting his home, I became aware that his father had previously divorced his mom. His mom had moved away with his brother and the other kids; practically, it was just him and his dad.

My earliest impression of my new friend was that he was too mature for his age. He used to run errands while his dad was at work, clean the house, cook, and did lots of other chores that I was not accustomed to doing. They lived in the community just one notch above ours. Their house had three bedrooms with toilet facilities inside the house.

By virtue of hanging out with him, I made friends with lots of other kids in his compound, including a girl who lived next door to his house who later became my first girlfriend. I was also now part of another soccer team. In addition, he introduced me to the Boy Scout Movement, where he was a troop leader. His leadership skills were quite outstanding at an early age. I reckoned that the experience of living alone with his dad had uniquely prepared him for life. Joe and Pat became my most trusted friends during my primary school years.

Not long after, I found out that Pat and his dad were staunch Jehovah's witnesses (Watch Tower Sect). They were known to go around spreading the gospel from door to door. Much as I did not share their faith, our friendship blossomed through the years, but before I continue with that journey, I wish to discuss the subject of religion and my earliest memories of what I experienced growing up.

There were quite a few churches in the town where I grew up. To the best of my recollection, most of the families in our town were churchgoers. Mostly, it was the mothers who took their kids to church. For the fathers, attending church was probably an optional undertaking. In our own family, my mother would take us to church every Sunday morning. My dad very rarely attended church. As a matter of fact, I did not think my father believed in God, but he made sure we attended church with mom. My mother was a deeply religious woman and very active in church matters, to the point that she became the leader of the women's organization.

For us children, attending Sunday school was something to look forward to. We were divided into groups by age and exposed to biblical stories, which I found very fascinating, such as the story of Daniel and his friends. There were also the stories of Joseph and Moses and how God used them in their respective journeys. It was mesmerizing, especially since our teacher was good at recounting these stories. Other than listening to biblical stories, we sang, played games, and several times in a year, performed sketches in front of the entire adult congregation. Every year we would be elevated to a new class in Sunday school, which made it even more interesting. I excelled in all my Sunday school quizzes and became my teachers' favorite student.

It was not long before I graduated from Sunday school and could now attend regular church with the rest of the adults. The church we attended was known as the United Church of Zambia. Attending church was quite an experience; our pastor was a Canadian man who had been sent as a missionary. He spoke the local language quite fluently, though his accent betrayed him many a time. He was supported by a group of elders we dubbed *Abena Korinto* (Corinthians), given that they looked so pious when they would step out of the backroom to start the service at 11:00 a.m. on Sunday. It was quite a spectacle to behold. When one of them would be asked to pray, they would take forever to say, "Amen." On a few occasions, someone in the congregation would shout "Amen!" to put an end to the prayer. Church services were segregated by sex; the men sat on the left side of the pews and the women on the right side. The explanation for this arrangement was to minimize distractions and temptation between the sexes. Despite this arrangement, the teen pregnancy rate in the church was quite high, especially among members of the choir.

As I grew older, it was not long before I began to understand and empathize with human weakness. Most of the folk who attended church had issues that were sometimes hidden from the rest of the congregation. The women's movement known as the KBBK was very active in monitoring teen pregnancies, and my mom was probably the most loyal member of this group. On one occasion, one of the daughters of an elder in the church was suspected of being pregnant. My mother was assigned to investigate the case. She gathered a group of women to the house to discuss the issue. A unanimous decision was made to ask the suspect to face the inquiry committee immediately. One of the women in the group went to fetch her and shortly afterward presented her to the group. After a series of obvious questions, she was asked to undress in the presence of all the women. She hesitated but did not really have a choice. They found out that she had been tightly wrapping a piece of cloth around her belly to hide the pregnancy. The next obvious question was who was responsible for her pregnancy. It turned out to be another member of the church, and the gossip spread like wildfire across the entire congregation. What was sad was that, in those days, pregnancy meant the end of a girl's academic pursuits. She would be segregated from school as an example to the other girls to emphasize the importance of chastity. The only available option for the girl would be to get married, but this was not always possible.

One occurrence that stuck with me for a long time was that of a very pious lady whom almost everyone in the church held in such high esteem. She had been to Bible College and was asked to serve the local church as an assistant in some capacity. She was very active in the church; no one disputed her credentials as a pillar in the community. Whenever she would be asked to pray, it was amazing how many congregants would tear up just listening to her prayers, myself included. However, she was a spinster and shared the church house with another family that also worked for the church.

At one point, she told the pastor that she was contemplating resigning. The pastor was vehemently opposed to this proposition. He suggested increasing her salary, but she was not buying the salary increase on the table despite the generosity of the offer. He finally gave up and asked her to announce to the rest of the congregation her decision to leave the church, which she did the following Sunday. Shortly before she left town, the rumor of her pregnancy began to gather steam. After the council of women got involved, it became apparent that the married man she shared the house with was responsible for her pregnancy. It was quite a scandal.

One other observation that I struggled with in this context was seeing teenage girls getting pregnant and having no recourse for correcting their supposed mistake. A pregnancy at the time amounted to a death sentence, if you consider that girls were not allowed to go back to school after getting pregnant. In that society, there were few options for success in life outside the academic path. You devoted yourself to studies as if your life depended on it. Ironically, it did. I recall the story of a girl in our neighborhood who got pregnant and was so desperate to terminate the pregnancy that she was willing to go to any length. She was advised to make a concoction of soap mixed with other illicit ingredients by presumably experienced street individuals. Somehow, she was able to terminate the pregnancy without her parents knowing about it. These were some of the common struggles that we observed growing up. I have to believe that somehow our young minds were affected by these and other observations.

The one event that brought the entire community together once every year was the celebration of our independence on October 24. It was such a joyous event that the entire community congregated in the local stadium to hear political speeches and, most importantly, to witness an array of cultural activities from all segments of society. Even more, there was also free food for everyone. We started the day by lining up in our respective schools and later marching in single file all the way to the stadium. One school after another would march past the podium where the governor and other ranking officials paraded in celebration. The primary schools would go first, followed by students from the one and only secondary school in town. Later, the workers from different government branches would follow and then the church groups and other communities.

When everyone was gathered, we would sing the four stanzas of the national anthem and then listen to boring political speeches, mostly centered on themes of constitutional legitimacy and how we became masters of our own destiny, which was quite ironic as we were not really free as a country. We still relied heavily on our colonial masters for the sustenance of our economy. Following all the boring speeches, the real fun would begin; exhibitions of local dances, sketches, games, and lots of food. My favorite event was called *nsale-nsale*, in which boys and girls were lined up on opposite ends by gender and asked on rotating turns to pick their favorite from the opposite sex while singing the nsale-nsale song. As much as I loved this event, I was rarely picked, diminishing my self-esteem with the opposite sex. At the end of the day, we were treated to displays of fireworks.

It was not all rosy growing up in my society. Too often, we were exposed to practices and behaviors not conducive to a healthy upbringing. The constant fighting between our parents that we witnessed, and the drunken behavior of our fathers left scars on our psyches that could have impaired us for life, except for the grace of God. I also had an uncle whom we looked up to as a role model. The man had a good job working for a local bank. He lived in a decent house and had a decent family of four daughters. On top of that, he had a car, which was quite a rare feat at the time. His wife was a sweet woman, but for whatever reason, he made the decision at some point to take on another woman—a mistress, I suppose. The explanation for this behavior from his perspective was that his wife could not give him a son. It was not long before the mistress conceived and bore him a daughter.

Too often, women were blamed for a lot of things they were not responsible for. There was also the story of another man in our community who wanted a son so badly that he ended up with eight girls before he sired a son. Feeding nine children then became a challenge he was not prepared for. Having a son in a society that discriminated against women seemed to make sense, but boys weren't always successful either and too often had a shorter life span compared to girls.

Funerals in Zambia deserve a special mention because they were quite a spectacle to behold. When someone died, the community rallied together to support the deceased family, but too often not in a good way. Most funerals were a true manifestation of how dysfunctional our society was. The squabbling that ensued even prior to the burial was unfortunate but avoidable; there was always someone in the family that wanted to know where the checkbook was amid the hype and confusion of a funeral. The family of the deceased was the one responsible for feeding the mourners, regardless of the length of the mourning period. Mourning periods of up to a month were not unusual, especially if relatives from the village did not show up in time. What fascinated me watching all this drama was the chaos that ensued when the relatives from the village would finally arrive. Even if no one was crying at the time, the women would rise up and go into a frenzy of wailing that was, to say the least, overwhelming.

Men were not supposed to cry; they were expected to take care of women overcome with emotion. As boys, we were taught not to cry. If your father saw you shedding tears, he would scold you in no uncertain terms—that is, if you were lucky enough not to be whacked. You were reminded as often as necessary that men did not cry. Simply put, we were supposed to control our emotions regardless of how we felt. As traumatic as it was to watch all the women wailing uncontrollably, we were expected to put up a straight, tough face and help console them.

The mourning would go on for twenty-four hours a day. When the women got tired of crying, they would sing until dawn to the point that everyone in the neighborhood was affected in one way or another. The expatriates who were unfortunate enough to live next to Zambian families soon began to complain about this practice, as they too could not sleep in the face of all the wailing and singing. It is uncertain how the individual complaints were resolved, but how do you tell people in mourning to keep quiet?

When it was time for the burial, there was a long procession, first to church and then to the cemetery. At church, there would be a service lasting approximately two hours, depending on how many people wished to say something about the deceased. After the church service, there would be another long procession to the cemetery, with more wailing and drama from close relatives begging to be buried with the deceased. That is when the men came in handy in terms of restraining the overly emotionally stricken women. After the burial, the majority would return to the funeral house, expecting to be fed. There were those who would make a career out of attending funerals; they figured out that this was a cheap means of making a living without too much effort. They would move without shame from one funeral to the next, pretending to be distant relatives until they were exposed. There was in consequence a song that was composed about unscrupulous men who would lie to their wives that they had been to a funeral when inquisitive spouses wanted to know where they had been the night before. It became a common joke to say that you had been to a funeral when someone asked where you had been but you did not wish to divulge the details of what you might have done.

I could not wait to grow up and start to forge a life of my own. Before I delve into the events that led me to my transition into adulthood, it is important that I discuss the general conditions and challenges that we faced as a young nation.

Fig 3: Mitobo Primary School in Kalulushi where my
long and winding academic journey was initiated

Fig 4: Entrance to the public swimming pool where I learned to swim

CHAPTER 3
The Nation at Large

Having attained political independence from Great Britain in 1964, Zambia faced several challenges, paramount of which were limited schooling opportunities. In the town where I grew up, for instance, there was only one secondary school serving four to five primary schools. The implication of this reality was that only a limited number of students were accepted into secondary school, regardless of how well they performed in the entrance examinations, which were conducted in the seventh grade of primary school. The students who made it went on to secondary school and those who did not had limited options.

For the majority, this marked the beginning of a death sentence. Faced with this reality, we were under much pressure to not only study hard but also to be selfish. The thought was that the guy you shared information with may just be the one who takes your place in secondary school, and therefore, you did whatever was within the realm of possibility to first take care of your own destiny. I learned to only share information and knowledge with friends within close circles. We would start preparing for the grade 7 exams as early as the fifth grade. We studied materials that were two to three grades above our own, all in the quest to leave no room for failing the much-dreaded grade 7 exams.

Not only were there limited opportunities for getting into secondary school, but also limited opportunities for finding work without a secondary school education. The educational system was such that you would spend seven years in primary school (grades 1–7), three years in junior secondary school (forms 1–3), and two years in senior secondary school (forms 4–5), with exams at each of the levels to determine whether you progressed or dropped out. Following secondary school, you would go to university for four or five years, depending on your major.

Probably the one opportunity you had if you did not make it into secondary school was to become a "yard boy," maintaining the homes of the upper-class folks, performing general maintenance tasks. At worst, you became a dropout with nothing else to do but rely on the mercy of relatives and friends. Those who dropped out of school at Form three had a few more options to explore but in general, even that was not good enough. If you completed secondary school but were not able to get into university, you could go to a technical college and learn a trade, which translated into some level of success with blue-collar jobs. At any cost, the goal was to get into university and that was drilled into your psyche from the moment you started primary school. If you were lucky enough, following the successful completion of high school, you were given a scholarship to study abroad, mostly in the UK. This was by far the preferred option that everyone worked toward. We propelled ourselves as much as possible to get to the top, where the air was much thinner. This meant studying almost every day, sometimes waking up early in the morning when everyone else was asleep. To avoid distracting those who would be sleeping at night, we would use a homemade improvised candle known as a *koloboi*.

The shortage of skilled manpower presented enormous challenges for a young nation such as ours. In almost every field, the folks who controlled the economy of the country were expatriates who ended up taking much of the foreign exchange that the country so desperately needed. Even in the teaching profession at secondary school, we had expatriate teachers who taught us the various subjects such as science, math, and English. Getting to the point of getting rid of foreign expertise was going to take a generation, but it also meant that for young Zambians who were willing to apply themselves, only the sky was the limit.

In terms of cultural aspects, it was apparent that while we had our own culture, Western influences were a distracting reality that could not be ignored. With the hippie movement of the 1970s coupled with Bruce Lee martial arts, we grew to like and copy whatever we saw from the west, thinking we were making progress in the right direction but in reality this was merely another manifestation of the identity crisis we faced. Marrying a white woman was what every boy dreamed of, even at a young age when we hardly understood the complex issues of race. This perpetuated a complex of inferiority. I remember seeing how mothers would patronize crying toddlers by telling them they were white and instantly the kids would stop crying. In school, white teachers were highly revered and preferred. There was also the issue of skin bleaching; products such as Ambi were highly in demand. Those who had a lighter skin complexion appeared to suffer from a superiority complex over those with darker skin tones. Women also did all they could to bring their hair closer to that of white women by using all sorts of chemical combinations. The issue was that we had no confidence in our own race; it was lamentable that we had lost our own identity in the name of progress.

When the bell-bottomed pants and balloon shirts were in vogue in the west, we did not wish to be left behind. We embraced music, especially by Black American and British singers such as Eddie Grant, Otis Redding, James Brown, and others. We grew to like everything foreign, not realizing that our culture was being eroded. There were also vices such as marijuana that we embraced because of our love for anything foreign. As we became of age in adolescence, I saw too many of the folks in our neighborhood get hooked on marijuana and drop out of school. In my own family, my older brother fell victim to the lure of marijuana and never quite found his way back, despite how much pressure my parents applied to correct his behavior.

One other challenge I observed growing up was based on language. Our parents came from different parts of the country and therefore they all spoke different languages. In Zambia, there are to this day about seventy-eight languages that are spoken. Understandably, there was a tendency to discriminate against others based on the language the parents spoke. This mentality pervaded much of the social structure.

Most of the time, jobs were awarded based on one's last name rather than for objective qualifications or the content of one's character. These were frustrations that we lived with as a young nation. Fortunately for the young generation, some of these entrenched behaviors were slowly beginning to fade away under the umbrella of "One Zambia, One Nation," espoused by the first president, Kenneth Kaunda.

The practice of witchcraft was quite prevalent in our society. To the young mind, unable to process issues objectively, witchcraft was a real source of fear; we heard a lot of stories about mysterious things that had happened to some folks through jealousy or conflict. One experience that was close to me was that of a distant relative who had said some unfortunate things to his mother. She retorted that while she was not strong enough to fight him, she would in due course take revenge. Shortly after that, his wife collapsed and died mysteriously. Subsequently, his eldest daughter passed away and then another daughter, all within a short space of time. He was still in mourning when he also collapsed and died. I also heard the story of a man who had been bitten by a snake and was rushed to a witch-doctor. Instead of giving the medicine to the victim of the snake bite, the witchdoctor started to gulp down some concoction and as he did, the poor victim began to recover. When the Zambian national soccer team lost a soccer match to Zaire in the early '70s, the major editorials of the two national newspapers at the time, both documented the possibility of foul play in the form of witchcraft. The one thing that intrigued me about witchcraft was that it only seemed to affect black people. I always used to wonder why it was not used against white people during the struggle for independence.

At a young age, the world can be quite a conflicting and confusing place. Reconciling all the issues one is exposed to can be quite a challenge. Prior to the age of ten, I had been exposed to so much that internally I did not know how to resolve anything. I tried to focus on school as much as I could and really believed that there was a path for me, no matter what obstacles I faced. The one constant in my life was the faith that my mom had introduced me to. Somehow, even though I had not embraced Christianity per se, I believed there was a God who was looking out for me despite the odds.

My years in primary school went by so quickly. I had been preparing for the grade 7 school-leaving exams for quite some time and was not in the least bothered by the possibility of a negative outcome. I was the best student in my class, and everyone expected nothing but excellent results from me. I was not overconfident, and neither was I pompous; I remained humble even in the face of all the praises that were lavished on me. On the designated date, I arrived in the exam room and focused on the work ahead. The supervisor began handing out preprinted answer sheets by name. Mysteriously, there was none for me and several other pupils in my class. We were instead given provisional answer sheets. This raised some concern on the part of those of us who were affected by this misfortune, considering that this was a national exam. This issue was duplicated for the rest of the subjects that we sat for, but this was a situation that was totally out of my control.

To cut a long story short, when the results came out, my name was not on the list of successful candidates transitioning to secondary school. All my close friends whom I used to study with had passed to move to secondary level and were jumping for joy. For the first time in my life, I had suffered the agony of failure. In that moment, I questioned God's existence and wondered why a loving God could allow this to happen to me. My mom was even more devastated, as I was the one who had showed more promise in relation to my siblings. Her agony and confusion were apparent, and so was mine. Being the woman of faith that she was, she would wake up every morning and pray for all of us, her children. When it was time to make supplications on my behalf before her father in heaven, she would break down crying, asking God for a special favor. On several occasions prior to that experience, I would hear her mention that I was the Joseph who had been consecrated to save the family. I certainly used to brush aside these assertions as wishful thinking, but such was the faith that sustained her. It appeared momentarily, though, that the dream was crushed. The pain from this experience would linger for quite some time. I could not see the path forward, but my uncle indicated that he would talk to one of the headmasters at another school regarding the possibility of repeating seventh grade.

The headmaster of the school was receptive to the idea, but he had received so many other requests from parents in similar situations. To make the process fair, he indicated that he was going to ask everyone interested in repeating grade 7 to take a test. He would only pick the five to ten top-scoring students. On the appointed day, more than two hundred candidates showed up. I was relieved to learn that I was one of the five students picked to repeat grade 7. At least, my mom was able to smile again. It would take another year before I would have a crack at the school leaver's exam again.

There were two individuals that contributed to my quick recovery during this trying period. One was a classmate whose friendship and counsel I truly valued. He lived in the section just below ours in the social hierarchy. The other individual was a girlfriend that one of my best friends from the next section had hooked me up with, as they were neighbors. The experience of being in puppy love with a girl for the first time helped to distract me from my pain. With hindsight, I do not know if it was love or merely a friendship with someone of the opposite sex. Coincidentally, she attended the same school where I had repeated seventh grade. I must have been eleven or twelve years at the time. She would walk with me from school, going home, and when no one was looking, we would hold hands. Both of us were quite shy at that age. I would confide in her, telling her how devastated I had been that my friends were now ahead of me, and she would respond asserting how unpredictable life could be sometimes. I would ask about her mom, whom I had never met. Sadly, her mom had passed away several years before and thereafter, she and her sister were sent to live with their uncle. I would respond expressing my sympathies. Sometimes we would talk about school; I would mention how determined I was to make it in secondary school. Her response was always encouraging. She was not a particularly gifted student, but she believed in me and reminded me to be grateful that I had been given another chance. She would then follow up the comment with something to the effect that if ever I made it in life, I should not forget about her. That was probably her way of expressing the insecurity she felt about her future. What better motivation did I need than that of a sweet girl as my cheerleader?

Whenever I did not see her for some time, I would write her letters on special paper labeled: "Forget Me Not." I would then pass the letters to one of her friends for delivery. Since they were never sealed, her friend would read the letters out of curiosity and later tease me on the contents. My letters would read something like this:

Dear ———,

I am so glad to have this chance to drop this short missive to you. I hope my missive finds you perambulating in good health. I think about you often and miss you. You are the sugar in my tea. Every time I see you, my heart goes *boom, boom, boom.* Do you know that love without sex is like tea without sugar?

Before I pen off, I want to say, "Sleep well, darling." Please do not let those bed bugs bite you. You are too sweet for them.

Yours very truly,

———

She would also write similar letters in return, which I kept securely and read over from time to time. We were in that age group when the mystery of sexual exploration occupied our thoughts twenty-four hours a day. Some of the boys within my circle of friendships were already relating stories of sublime sexual encounters. The peer pressure not to be left behind was enormous.

One day, while walking from school with my sweetie pie, I found the courage to raise the poignant question to try it out. To my surprise, she raised no objections. We agreed to meet after dark at the housing office clad with well-manicured lawns, located across the street from our house. I got there first and waited for what seemed like an eternity. She finally showed up, wearing a *chitenge* (loose) cloth around her waist, but I had no idea what to say or do next. I was such a nervous wreck, sweating bullets all over my body. Sensing my lack of experience, she practically took over and walked me through the entire experience. She was only a year older than me but was certainly more mature. I sensed that she had been with another boy before. To my surprise, the episode was over in less than three minutes. All I recall was "speaking in tongues" out of sheer ecstasy, and then I was back to my normal senses. We stood up and walked home; our sweaty bodies wrapped in each other's arms but engulfed in silence and what I perceived to be deep embarrassment. My only consolation was that now I had something to brag about with my peers.

My teacher in my new school was a rather energetic and nice man; he was very talkative and liked to discuss the politics of the day. He grew to trust my friend and me to the extent that he would invite us to his home to run errands for him. Occasionally, he would ask us to help him grade the class tests, which we considered an honor. Sometimes he would also invite two other girls to his house to do house chores for him as his wife was also a schoolteacher and hardly found the time to catch up on housework. They would leave the four of us in their house for extended periods of time. We cherished the experience of having the freedom to interact with the opposite sex in a secluded environment. This was a privilege that every teenager would have relished. For the record, we were on our best behavior in the teacher's house.

The year went by so very quickly. Before long, it was time to sit for the grade 7 exams again. I had done my best to prepare, but this time, I was somewhat nervous, not being sure what the outcome would be. This time around, I had preprinted answer sheets, unlike the previous time. I knew my mom was praying for me. We wrote the exams in early December and then began the long wait for the results in January.

My mom was friends with the wife of the headmaster at the local secondary school. When the results were reported, copies were also sent to the secondary school. On the eve of the results being posted, the wife of the headmaster paid us a visit to give us the news that not only had I passed this time but also that I had done so well that the honor of being sent to a technical boarding school for academically gifted kids was being extended to me. By coincidence, she had a son who was attending the same technical secondary school already. Little did I know that her son would turn out to be my best friend for all the time I would spend in my new school. I was not home when my mom's friend showed up. My mom resisted giving me the news until the following morning and cautioned me not to tell anyone until the results were posted. She was happy and relieved. I immediately set off, heading toward the primary school. The only news for discussion that day had to do with the grade 7 school leavers' results. As I drew closer to the school, people I never knew were pointing at me, saying, "That's him." Consequently, I was able to confirm the outcome.

To say that I was elated was an understatement. Neighbors came to congratulate me on this rare feat, and so did my friends who were already in secondary school. My girl sent a note, congratulating me with the reminder that I should not forget the promise I had made to her. I took a walk around the neighborhood, trying to digest what had just happened. It was too much to put in perspective. In His own way and on His timing, the good Lord had found a way to soothe a broken heart. Little did I know that this was only the first in a series of events that He would use to mold me to His liking and impart a powerful lesson. Like He did to Moses, He had brought me to a place of complete surrender where I had no choice but learn to trust him completely. It was as if the Almighty, whose existence I had questioned the year prior, was now inquiring of me like He did to Job (in the Bible) whether I was capable of instructing Him in His ways or if I was there when He laid the foundations of the earth and caused the light to part from darkness, when he said to the seas, "You can only come this far." Whatever I had uttered the year prior was all in ignorance. Certainly, I could not contend with Him. Oh, the depth of the riches of His wisdom and knowledge! How unsearchable are His judgements and His ways past finding out! For who has known the mind of God to instruct Him? For from Him and through Him and to Him are all things, and to Him be the glory forever. Amen!

Up to this day, this was the fundamental experience that I have kept going back to in the face of adversity and doubt as a reminder that when God is on your side, nothing or no one can stand in the way. It was a powerful lesson that only the Almighty could impart to a young lad who had once thought his dreams had been shattered.

CHAPTER 4
High School Experiences

I hastily began to make arrangements to travel to my new school with much excitement. My new school was located about a thousand kilometers from where we lived, and travel by train was the cost-effective alternative. The trip would take almost twenty-four hours on the Luangwa train, as it would stop at multiple stations along the way. My mom accompanied me on the trip, but I was not really thrilled with this arrangement. Upon boarding the train, I came to discover that there were two other students on the train heading to the same school. One of the students was accompanied by his older sister, while the other one was on his own. We quickly bonded in friendship, and so did my mother and the other lady. Being in a group with other folks heading for the same destination helped to ease the anxiety associated with the trip.

Having left at night, we arrived in Lusaka, the capital city, the following morning. It was the first time in my life that I had been to Lusaka. I was fascinated with the high-rise buildings in the distance. What a blessing this experience was turning out to be. We left Lusaka and proceeded to Kafue and then into the southern province, which was the final stretch to Livingstone. We arrived late in the evening, and the five of us took a cab to Hillcrest, our new school. We were met by the head boy of the school, who immediately arranged for my mom and the other lady to sleep in a campus house that was vacant. The rest of us were directed to our preassigned dormitories, where we were introduced to the dorm captains. The dorm captains were students in the senior forms who were tasked with maintaining discipline and order. I was directed to house 7; my other colleagues were sent to houses 2 and 4. In the moment, I experienced separation anxiety from my new friends.

The dorm captain, who turned out to be a nice guy, showed me around the dorm and asked me to pick a place where I wanted to sleep. I chose a location close to the entrance for no specific reason. I was assigned a locker and then introduced to the folks I would be sharing my cubicle with. The student in the upper bunk bed lowered himself from his bed, extending his hand of friendship with a big smile. I shook his hand, introducing myself. I noticed that he was disabled, but he put me at ease very quickly; he helped me unpack my bag and make my bed. Very quickly, we clicked and became good friends. We chatted a little, and then it was lights out. I can't remember if I slept that first night, but I was exhausted.

The ritual in boarding school was that we woke up at the same time every morning and proceeded to the ablution block to clean ourselves up, and then the bell for breakfast would ring. One was expected to be in the dining hall within a given time frame. Failure to present oneself at the dining hall within the specified time frame meant the choice to skip breakfast voluntarily. Once the prefects shut that door, there was no other recourse. We followed the other students through this ritual on our first day. Breakfast was a cup of tea, a slice of bread, and porridge. After breakfast, I checked on my mom. She was doing just fine. The head boy had arranged for their breakfast. It was Saturday morning, and nothing much was going on that day. Lots of the other students were arriving by the hour. Before long, there were quite a few of us. Student orientation was probably the only thing going on for us. We kept ourselves busy walking around the campus, getting to know where everything was. I was happy to note that there was a swimming pool on campus, where I could perfect my swimming skills. In addition, there were two or three soccer fields, a basketball court, and several tennis and volleyball courts at our disposal.

My mom left the following morning on Sunday. Prior to her departure, she prayed with me and handed me a Bible, saying to me, "I hope you make us proud, my son." It was the best gift I had ever received from her. Following a few words of wisdom, she quickly disappeared from my sight in a cab. Seeing her leave was not easy, but I had prepared myself for this moment. For the first time in my life, I was away from home and on my own. However, all things considered, it was a blessing, as I was being exposed to something that the rest of my siblings would have so much desired to have. I was certainly apprehensive, not knowing what the future portended. As the Chinese proverb goes, even the longest of all journeys must begin with the first step. This was my first step; I was determined to make the best of it.

We started school the following day, Monday. After breakfast, we went back to our dorms for morning inspection. A prefect came by to verify that we were compliant with the dress code and other general rules of conduct. Following inspection, it was time to proceed to the assembly hall, where the headmaster and the teachers would find us. The teachers came in first and took their positions behind the podium. When the head master finally walked in, everyone stood up to sing the national anthem and one of the students was asked to read a prayer. The headmaster then proceeded to welcome the new students and made other pertinent announcements. He was a stern-looking man who wore a turban owing to his Indian heritage.

I was assigned to form 1B class. Before our first teacher arrived, we got busy getting to know our classmates and learning where they were from. We all came from different parts of the country, and therefore, there was a lot to learn from each other and talk about. We met our first teacher, who I did not think was very nice; he came across as rude and very dictatorial. When it was time to go to another class, we had our first encounter with bullying. Some of the students in the higher grades would scratch our faces as a form of mockery, or perhaps it was a form of welcome. My understanding was that mockery or bullying was more like an initiation of some sort and was meted out to all new students. Being new, we had no appetite to fight back. The mockery went on for several weeks, and then it just fizzled away. Before long, I was getting accustomed to boarding school life and all its formal routines consisting of classes, meals, recreational activities, cleaning, independent studies, and final roll call in the dorms before lights out. Such was the discipline in boarding school, intended to instill values that contributed to making us independent.

Every Saturday morning, we had to do house cleaning activities. The dorm captains assigned us our responsibilities early in the morning, which consisted of either cleaning inside the dorms or in the ablution block or attending to the flower beds around the dorms. A serious inspection followed the cleaning activities. The head boy and his two deputies conducted this inspection and awarded points such that the best house for the week was recognized during assembly on the following Monday.

On Saturdays, we had mandatory study in the mornings, but the afternoons were free. We used that time to do laundry and other recurring chores. For those of us who were bookworms, this was the time to gain that advantage over the other students. Sundays were personal days. We could go to church as we pleased. Before long, I had hooked up with some friends, attending church regularly as a group. One of them turned out to be the boy from my town who was the son of the headmaster at the local secondary school. He became like a brother to me. Unlike me, he spoke fluent English, given the privileges he had been exposed to—living on the other side of town and mingling with the expatriates' kids. There were other kids at my new school who spoke impeccable English; they were mostly from Lusaka (the capital city). Their parents were well-to-do, and therefore, they had enjoyed the privileges of being sent to the best private schools that money could buy. These "elite" kids mingled by themselves most of the time and were not always friendly to the rest of us. They had plenty of pocket money; their lockers were filled with all kinds of delicacies to supplement their diet. To be in the same class and brushing shoulders with them was like leveling the playing field. In our new environment, our differences were not that pronounced. My mind was slowly opening to the ingrained structural imbalances at the national level. Fortunately, or unfortunately, in the game of life, one can only play the hand that he is dealt. However, at some point, we all become responsible for shaping our own destiny, regardless of our parents' status. This I understood quite early in my life, and I became more determined than ever to do my best, as school was likely my only avenue to success.

One of the things I grew to like in boarding school was watching movies on Saturday nights. We were treated to all kinds of fun movies ranging from Westerns to action-packed thrillers. Any movie with a hint of sex always drew wild cheers from a bunch of teenagers with raging hormones. On some Saturdays, in lieu of movies, we were treated to variety shows organized by the drama club. The shows consisted of a wide array of entertainment activities, such as plays, sketches, magic, and so forth. Some of the plays we watched in our first year were quite captivating. One that I have never forgotten to this day was a production entitled "Soweto," depicting the struggle for independence in Apartheid South Africa. I was exposed to and learning so many things so fast that it was hard to keep up. I could not wait to go home for the holidays to recount the marvels I was experiencing in school.

It was not long before one of my friends suggested a visit to the mighty Victoria Falls. I had heard so much about the Victoria Falls, as it was one of the seven natural wonders of the world, and could not wait to see it. Attending school in the tourist capital of the country was a privilege without parallel. When the time came, a few of us put together a few kwachas (the local currency) and hired a cab. The trip took about forty minutes, and as we got closer to the falls, we could see monkeys and other small animals running around. The driver dropped us off at one of the local hotels that was a short walking distance to the location of the falls. The noise of water falling from a great height was deafening. Wearing our school uniforms, we trusted and followed the lead of the students who had been there before. The suggestion was to start by walking over the knife-edge bridge from where we could see the Zambezi river descend off a cliff. We hastened to the bridge, my little heart pounding with so much excitement. Before we could even get to the bridge, we were drenched; the mist from the waterfall was overwhelming. We could hardly hear each other talk, but we kept walking until we reached the bridge. When we turned around to see the falls, there were a series of rainbows that created a spectacular view. It was so uplifting. We kept walking toward the Rhodesian (Zimbabwe) side of the falls, but we could only go until the demarcation point, given that the struggle for the liberation of Southern Rhodesia was still a work in progress across the border. We turned around at the point where we could go no farther and then headed to the bottom of the falls, known as the boiling pot.

When the water falls from such a great height, it churns continuously, creating the illusion of boiling water, hence the name. Seeing this natural wonder was a sublime experience that I could never forget. When we thought we had seen it all, our group leader suggested a walk to the Maramba village to watch African dances. This was a nearby spot where most tourists used to congregate to take a break from watching the falls. The entertainment was a showcase of culture and was not disappointing; we loved every moment of it. It was almost 4:00 p.m. when we decided to go back to school. This was an experience that I would live to cherish for the rest of my life. That evening, I decided to write letters to my parents and some of my closest friends. I wrote that I was very happy in my school and that not only was I learning academics but that there were also so many other things I was exposed to that enriched my life. Needless to say, I recounted the wonders of the Victoria Falls in all my letters. A few weeks later, when I got the responses, I was all smiles.

Three months went by quickly, and we wrote our end of term exams. I ranked third in class overall. One of the boys from Lusaka topped the class during the first trimester. I knew I could have done better, but overall, it wasn't a bad start.

We boarded the train in the evening and headed home but not until some schoolmates had had the chance to make up for the drinks they had skipped over a three-month period. This was the opportunity to get drunk, misbehave, and curse the teachers who had made our lives so miserable. Some of the kids from the more affluent families boarded the faster train which left during the morning hours. There was a lot of fun on the train; what made it even more interesting was that girls from another boarding school in the same town were also on board the train. This was the time to impress and hook up with a girl, if you could. Unfortunately for me, I was a little goofy with the opposite sex and therefore was not successful for the entire trip, at least not this time around. The most my friend and I had managed was talk to one girl and her sister. They were very friendly and seemed to have good morals.

We reached our destination just before nightfall the following day. My friend's father picked us up at the train station. Approximately thirty minutes later, they dropped me off at my parents' house to a motivated and cheering welcoming committee consisting of family, friends and even some curious onlookers. I felt like the prodigal son. My mom was the loudest cheerleader and rightly so; this was a proud moment for her, and she could not contain her emotions. She hugged me and did not want to let go for quite some time. While she was hugging me, she was uttering psalms of praise to her ancestors who had made this moment possible. When she finally let go of me, I reached into one of my bags for a photo album, which I had acquired to share with them my experiences in my new school. When they saw images of me standing in front of the falls, there were gasps and almost tears of disbelief. News that I had arrived was beginning to spread, and neighbors came around to welcome one of their own. I had instantly become a role model, an example to the community of what was possible. My young brother was so impressed with me that he kept asking questions, including ones I did not have answers to. In moments like this, I reminded myself that I needed to guard against the instinct of pride. As one of my teachers had taught me just the prior trimester, I ought to take the position of "There go I but for the grace of God."

During the one-month holiday, I found time to help my parents harvest ground nuts, maize, sweet potatoes, and beans. Since land was in abundance, the city government used to allocate farming land to every willing family. We would wake up early in the morning and walk for more than two hours to get to our plot (kumabala). My mom would usually pack something to eat and drink. This was probably motivation for my brothers and me; if you chose not to go, it simply meant there would be nothing else at home to eat. Other than helping with chores around the house, I found time to catch up or get ahead in my studies. I was not too happy with my results in math the prior trimester, and so, in order to brush up, I spent some time with my former schoolmates who were attending the local secondary school. I picked up some very helpful tips from them and explored some material they were covering in the second year—the level ahead of mine. I enquired after my girlfriend but was disappointed to learn that she was spending time with another boy. It was time to move on.

On Sundays, I started attending another church where the services were conducted in English. This was the church my school friend Dumi attended regularly when he was home. Subsequently, I became very good friends with a girl (Mary) of my age who lived close to my neighborhood and had started attending the same church too. We became very close, but there was nothing romantic going on between us. Our parents knew each other, so she was free to visit as she pleased. I in turn would visit her house without prior notice. Her mom had a liking for me and jokingly called me her son-in-law. It was the first time that I had ever been in a genuine friendship with a member of the opposite sex.

I returned to school when the holidays were over to start the second trimester of my first year in secondary school. Nothing much of significance transpired during this period. I was very focused on my studies and did not allow anything to distract me. My goal was to excel in my class and subsequently, at the end of the trimester, I had risen to top of the class. I stayed in that position until the end of my third year, when we took the form 3 exams. The strategy of studying with my friends (who were a year ahead of me) during the holidays was paying off handsomely.

My second year was probably the most interesting of my boarding school years. My history teacher turned out to be a Jewish American who had joined the peace corps and found his way to Zambia. He was quite a good teacher who made history interesting; he was always looking for ways to motivate us. One day, he put an offer on the table. The offer was that whoever was going to be the first to solve a crossword puzzle would get a prize consisting of a loaf of bread. Since bread was a staple food in boarding school, we all started working on the puzzle as soon as the papers were handed out. I finished mine in about five minutes and looked around, but everyone was busy. I raised my hand and handed over the answers to the quiz. I was declared the winner as jeers of disgust ran through the entire classroom. The following week, the same teacher gave us an assignment to research the life of the prophet Mohammed. I went to the library and did extensive research, which I presented to the class as soon as the teacher asked for volunteers.

I had captured my teacher's attention; we developed a close bond. I used to ask him a lot of questions about America, and he never got tired of answering questions about his country. The sad thing is that at the end of the trimester, he decided to move to Lusaka for another teaching position at an international school. It was sad to see him go, but he left me his address and phone number in case I wanted to get in touch. Whenever I would write him letters, he was quick to respond without reservations. At the end of the second trimester, he asked me to stop for a visit in Lusaka on my way home, which I did, but I had no clue as to what a surprise I was in for. He picked me up at the train station. From there, we headed straight to one of the best hotels in the city, where we ordered lunch. I still remember to this day what I ordered: chicken in the basket; a comfort food at its finest. Following lunch, we headed to his home, where I met his wife and two children.

In the evening, he treated me to another surprise—dinner at a restaurant on the top floor of another very modern hotel, after which we were entertained by a live band. He introduced me to all his friends who were there too. Some, I recall, were Japanese. I was simply overwhelmed. To find myself in places that I could previously only dream of was a little confusing. In such a short span of time, I had been exposed to so much that I could not make sense of what was going on in my life. I knew I had done nothing to deserve his favor.

We returned to the apartment, and before retiring to bed, he handed me what looked like a small brochure. I started to look at it but was not sure what I was looking at. I turned the page over, and there was my name written inside. It was an air ticket to fly from Lusaka to Kitwe the following day. How did I say thank you to a man who had treated me with so much kindness? It was beyond belief. The following day, he drove me to the airport and walked me through the necessary routines. He directed me to the waiting room and excused himself as he had an engagement with his wife and so had to leave. I thanked him for his kindness and sat down to wait for my flight. It was the first time I was going to fly. Undoubtedly, I was a bit apprehensive, not knowing what to expect. The flight attendant helped me with my seat belt, and that was it. The plane took off without any glitches. I looked outside the window admiring the landscape for much of the flight time as I digested what had become of my life. Life did not make much sense at all, but if this was God's favor upon my life, I was surely going to embrace it.

Upon my arrival in Kitwe, I took a Zamcab (taxi) home, and when I showed up in a cab at that hour, my mom looked perplexed. Her first question as she attempted to hug me was "Where did you get the money to be riding in a cab?" When I explained what had happened, she was silent for a moment and uttered something I could not quite grasp. I took it that she was thanking the God of heaven for the confirmation of the vision of hope He had placed upon her heart. In that moment, I recalled the story of Joseph that she used to recount to us when we were kids. She truly believed in her heart of hearts that I would grow up to be the "Joseph" of the family.

Upon my return to school the following trimester, Dumi invited me to a Scripture Union (SU) meeting. SU was a Christian organization that was established with the goal of helping young people in secondary school to continue to pursue their Christian faith. The group used to meet once a week to read and discuss the Bible. We also sang and formed a choir. Most of us used to attend the same church on Sunday, so occasionally we were called upon to sing in Church. One of the teachers was assigned to lead the group as patron. I was excited to join, and I met quite a few other young people with similar beliefs. It was refreshing to meet young people so dedicated to the ministry of spreading the gospel of Jesus Christ to other young folks.

The SU organization used to host camps for young people in several places around the country during the first week of the holidays. Dumi suggested that we should consider attending, especially since it would be an opportunity to meet girls from other parts of the country. We were at that age in life where meeting girls was a morale booster, and I did not hesitate in the least. We decided to sign up for the camp in Lusaka. I wrote to my parents asking for money to attend; they were quite supportive in sponsoring my trip. I was cognizant they were making huge sacrifices in the family budget to accommodate my request. I could not wait for the end of trimester.

We travelled to camp by train as usual. At the train station, we were picked up by a van that took us to camp, about forty minutes' drive away. The site was quite beautiful. The organization had acquired the property from a previous farmer. There were dormitory buildings for men and women, a dining area, toilet facilities, playgrounds, and other amenities. There was a creek that ran across the property, which supplied our water needs. There must have been more than a hundred young people congregated in this location. We were greeted by so many smiling faces, both female and male, and I felt very welcome. It was a blast from the get-go; the singing was almost nonstop. When someone picked up a tune to sing, someone else would join in and then another. Before long, there would be a group of "brothers" and "sisters" praising the Lord in unison. Anyone who had a song to share could do so with advanced notice and would be added to the program. The excitement I experienced was something I had never felt before. It was obvious that the love of God was among the camp attendees. We would start the day with morning prayers, then physical exercises, followed by breakfast, Bible study, games, lunch, personal time, group Bible study, more games, and dinner.

After dinner, we would have a guest speaker who would preach every night for the duration of camp. Prior to the preaching of the Word, we would hear from a brother or sister (in Christ) who would give a testimony on how they came to meet the Lord. Some of the testimonies were quite moving. It was all to demonstrate that no matter where you have been, Jesus loves you and is calling you back home. When the weather was promising, we would have the evening program around a campfire, which made it even more relaxing. You could look up into the sky and behold the bright stars and moon in the distance while you listened to the preaching of the Word, enjoying the warmth of the fire. The setting was just perfect.

It was on the second night that I heard the gospel of Christ presented in a way that turned my life around. The guest preacher started with a word of prayer, read a few biblical verses, and then introduced the theme for the night. It was Salvation 101. He posed the following question to the audience: "How do you know you are saved?" He was one of those fire-and-brimstone preachers who captivated his audience by controlling his intonation, speaking loudly when he needed to make a point and lowering his voice to make a plea for souls. At the end of the preaching, someone broke into the famous hymn: "Just as I am, without one plea." Everyone joined in the chorus; it was quite a moving moment. He proceeded to close in prayer and later indicated that he would be around to pray with anyone and make additional clarifications for anyone in need. The conviction of the Holy Spirit was so real for me. For the first time, I understood that I had merely been practicing religion without a personal relationship with Christ. I wanted to talk to the preacher-man so badly, but there were many others congregated around him.

I felt a genuine need to pray and ask God for the forgiveness of my sins. A thought crossed my mind to head for the toilet area, where there was no one. I went into one of the stalls and instantly began to pray. I came out a changed soul. I looked for my friend and recounted to him what I had experienced. He was overjoyed; we prayed together and encouraged each other to not keep the fire to ourselves but to go around and tell others about the love of God. I had found what had eluded me for so long—the peace of mind and quietness of heart that comes with walking with God. I just wanted to proclaim to every living being that Christ is the answer, and I did.

At the end of that one-week camp, we went home to spend the rest of the holidays with our families. When I got home, I did not hesitate. I started talking to all my friends and family about the plan of salvation. Sometimes, I would team up with my friend, and we would go "witnessing," as we used to call it. There were some who listened, and others who did not. We simply watered but also understood that it was Christ who gave the increase. We returned to school with the same agenda—to tell everyone about the love of God. We were just getting started. We were on fire for Jesus. It was not long before everyone in school began to notice that there was a spiritual movement going on.

We started meeting every night after supervised study for prayer meetings. We started off as a small group, but within a few weeks, our numbers began to grow; our plan was to encourage everyone to bring someone new every night. We would sing, pray together, and have one of us share something from the Bible. We wasted no time; we preached the gospel at every opportunity we were given. Our numbers were now in the hundreds, and we needed a bigger class-room. One of my dormmates I had the chance to witness to was a young man by the name of Chiluba. He and I bonded in friendship as he gave his life to Christ. He became one of my closest confidants for the duration of my secondary school years. The good Lord kept increasing our numbers, and we were so overwhelmed, but we never tired of or shied away from telling others about the love of God. This spiritual awakening in the late '70s was not just at my school but across the country. Young people were turning their lives around by embracing the message of the cross.

It was not long before some of the prefects at school began to complain that those of us who were attending prayer meetings at night were not adhering to the school rule associated with being in bed at a set time. While we had lobbied for an exemption for those attending prayer, there were some students who were using prayer meetings as a pretext not to be in bed at the specified time. The headmaster took measures to temporarily stop prayer meetings until the situation was under control. We understood this to be an attack from the very abyss of hell. We were not deterred; this time around, we had reason to start fasting. At one point, we fasted for seven days without eating anything. We were prepared to do anything just to see someone added to the fold. We called this the passion for souls.

Around this same time, the quality of the food in the dining hall continued to deteriorate. At one point, we ate *nshima* (a Zambian staple consisting of a thick porridge made by mixing water and corn-meal) and beans for about twenty-one days in a row. No amount of pleading with the boarding master made any difference; we had at the time a black headmaster who was probably not well respected. The Indian headmaster we had found when we first arrived had been transferred to another school. Some of the students in the senior forms mobilized the pupils to stage a protest by not showing up for meals or classes. The headmaster tried to talk the students out of it, but no one budged. The situation got so tense that when it was nightfall, a law enforcement brigade was brought in. To announce their arrival, they fired several blank shots in the air, and we all scattered in different directions, exiting the campus. I stayed in proximity to my brothers in the faith. Around 10:00 p.m., scouts were sent to survey the situation on campus. The law enforcement brigade was still around, but the headmaster had made a passionate plea using a loudspeaker, requesting all students to retire to bed. We reluctantly headed to our dorms but stayed awake, not quite knowing what was going to happen next.

At daybreak, the dining hall bell rang, and everyone rushed to the dining hall as we were all hungry. The first riot in the history of the school had ended, and it was back to business. What we did not know was that behind the scenes, a list of ringleaders was being compiled. Those in form 3 who were due to take their exams at the end of the year did so without knowing that they would not be going back if they were on the list. For the students in other forms, they too were allowed to finish the year before being told that they were expelled.

Following these measures, there was no further appetite for riots. I entered the third year determined to put in the extra effort to ensure a successful transition to the senior years. It was a common habit for most students preparing for exams to wake up around 3:00 a.m. and study until 6:00 a.m. The reality was that we were competing against one another; only the top three classes out of six would make it to the senior forms. Nothing eventful really happened that year; it was just the usual routine. I had started to play chess earlier on but slowed down in my third year to ensure it was not a distraction.

Toward the end of November, we started the exams. Exams were taken in the assembly hall to minimize the possibility of cheating, except for the technical classes such as woodwork, metalwork, and technical drawing. We took one exam every day until completion, with a total of nine subjects. We finished the exams during the first week in December; it was such a big relief not to feel the weight of the tests on our shoulders. We packed our bags and headed to the train station as usual. The drinking and vomiting that followed was not a surprise to anyone anymore. We went home and waited for our fate. By the second week in January, we would all receive letters informing us whether we would be going back or not. I got mine; I would be going back. However, there was no breakdown of how well I had fared in the exams. Those details would be available upon my return to school.

I was pleasantly surprised upon returning to school to be informed that I was one of two students who had scored As in all nine subjects. As a result, my name would be etched on the most coveted honor roll. Once again, the good Lord had proved himself faithful. I was now looking at just two years before completing secondary school.

My last two years in secondary school were probably the best of my life in Zambia. As a senior, I moved into the senior dormitories, which were housed in a three-story building with additional amenities that were not available to juniors. It also meant that I got to wear trousers (pants), a long-sleeved shirt, and a tie for my uniform in lieu of the pair of shorts and short-sleeved shirt I wore as a junior. The senior classrooms were also located in a different section, further from the noise and bustle of the juniors. I was ecstatic starting my fourth year. All my teachers turned out to be the very best I could ever wish for. Math was my favorite subject; it was probably the only subject in which I never allowed anyone to excel over me. In the weekly quizzes, I was almost always top of the class.

Not only was I involved in academics, but I also participated extensively in civic organizations. For starters, I was chosen to be a member of the Rotary Club. This was a rare honor reserved only for top-achieving students. I was asked to serve as vice president on the executive committee. Our mission was simple—to foster fraternity and goodwill in our communities. As a student chapter, we engaged in fundraising activities and used the money to give back to the community through various projects. We also held parties and invited students from the girls' school. Getting the girls to come was no easy feat; their headmistress, who was responsible for approving the meetings, was a tough nut to crack. She rarely allowed the girls to visit the boys' school unless it was for a compelling reason.

About once a year, we met with the local chapter, usually at one of the local hotels. This was an event to look forward to, mostly because the buffet dinner was a good break from the usual school diet of nshima and beans. As a matter of fact, despite the protests of the two prior years, the school diet never quite improved. The official response was that the cash-strapped government was not allocating further resources to the secondary schools. We were told to consider ourselves lucky that we did not have to pay for our education, boarding, and food. Our only recourse was to be resourceful and find ways to supplement our diet. Two of my best friends (Dumi and Chiluba) and I formed an association we dubbed Azid and Loe. The acronym stood for the Association of Zikolo Drinkers and Loaf Eaters. Bread, for us, was a staple food. Zikolo was nothing more than a concentrated mixture of sugar and water in a one-to-one approximate ratio by volume. It was highly concentrated and sweet, and that is not sugarcoating it. In the school dining hall, we would only get a slice of bread each, which was never enough. We would therefore put our pocket money together and use it to buy bread and sugar. These two staples were "golden" and highly coveted. Lockers were sometimes broken into in search of these precious commodities. Having a bottle of Zikolo and bread prior to bedtime was all a hungry student could ever ask for.

Other than the Rotary Club, I was also very engaged in Scripture Union activities as vice chair. While I did not formally join the Chess Club, I used to play chess occasionally, though sometimes I tended to overdo it. There were times we would play chess games that did not end until the following day. I would go to bed thinking about my next move, and this turned out to be a big distraction from the things I really needed to focus on. One of our mates had the honor of representing the southern region at the national level chess tournament, competing for a spot at the international level, but unfortunately, he lost in the final game.

In my senior years, a colleague and I had the opportunity to represent our school in the science quiz and won second place. Unfortunately, this was not good enough to move to the national level. There was also the East/Central and Southern African Mathematics Problem Contest that I had the honor of participating in during my fourth year. There were probably about twenty African countries that participated in this event, which consisted of mathematical puzzles that tested one's ability to translate and apply mathematical knowledge to solve complex real-life issues. I ranked thirty-third out of approximately a thousand students. It was not an outstanding result, considering that one of my classmates ranked third overall. He was one of the boys from Lusaka who was in constant rivalry with me for the top position in the class.

I continued to attend Scripture Union camps as often as I had the ability to. During one of those trips, I ran into a girl who used to live in a nearby town but had relatives living in mine. We became friends and exchanged addresses with the promise that she could visit anytime she was in town. Her name was Glenda. It is unfortunate that cell phones did not exist then, but true to her promise, one day during the holidays, when she was visiting her aunty, she showed up at my home unexpectedly. I was inside, but my mom was outside when she arrived. She boldly approached my mom and asked for me. That was not exactly a common scene at the time. A girl going to a guy's house and having the nerve to ask the mother for her son was at best a form of disrespect and, at worst, a confrontation. My mom just was not sure how to respond to a very elegantly dressed and confident young lady. Somehow, she took the polite option of asking my sister to let me know that I had a visitor.

In the meantime, she proceeded to ask my friend a series of probing questions. It was almost an interrogation of some sort, creating an awkward situation for the poor girl. I rushed outside to meet her and introduced her as one of the girls I had previously attended SU camp with. She was quite relieved to see me, as she was getting very uncomfortable with the line of questioning my mom had initiated. I invited her inside, where we sat down, but there were others in the sitting room, and so she did not talk much. I sensed the awkwardness and quickly created an excuse for us to leave. After I had escorted her, I confronted my mom, stating that her line of questioning was inappropriate and that she had embarrassed my friend, who had no motives for paying me a courtesy visit. It was clear from that day onward that I was no longer a kid. I let my mother know that sooner or later, I would be bringing her a daughter-in-law and therefore she needed to get used to the idea.

Before I returned to school that holiday, Glenda invited me to her parents' house, where I was warmly welcomed by her mom. In contrast, they lived in an affluent neighborhood (*kuma yadi*). It turned out that her mom was outstandingly nice; we had Bible study, and the mom chose to join us. I shared a few biblical verses of encouragement, speaking for about five to ten minutes. Her mom was very impressed with me and later excused herself to start preparing lunch for us. We were not dating as such, but I started entertaining a few ideas of my own about possible future permutations and combinations. She was quite an attractive girl, to be candid.

In the last trimester of my fourth year, I was appointed to serve as prefect. Prefects were essentially teachers' representatives tasked with enforcing discipline and maintaining order. The responsibility came with certain privileges, such as having a room instead of sleeping in the dorms. Rooms were generally shared with another prefect, but I was lucky enough to get one where I was the sole occupant. In addition to that, prefects were free to leave campus at almost any time, as long as they wore the school uniform. We had a lot of privileges, and the authority to ensure discipline was enforced. Another perk that came with this added responsibility was something we commonly referred to as "top soup," whereby whenever food was prepared, the first servings were reserved for prefects, with portions larger than for the rest of the students. This, for obvious reasons, did not sit well with the other students. Prefects were generally despised as it was thought that they did not represent the interests of the general student population. Being a strict disciplinarian, I had my fair share of confrontations with other students, but that came with the territory.

I completed the fourth form without too many issues. At the same time, the students I had started primary school with had just completed their fifth form exams, so there was really no one to study with when I got home for the six-week Christmas holiday. I found the time to study on my own, as well as engage in other meaningful initiatives to keep busy. I was pleasantly elated to learn that my young brother had become a Christian through my influence. He saw my life of prayer, dedication, and focus on school, ultimately coming to the conclusion that God was in control of my life. Whatever I had, he wanted the same for himself. That I did not know at the time. It was only much later that I had the opportunity to hear his testimony of how he came to embrace the message of the cross. Either way, I was thankful that my prayers had been answered.

As for my older brother, he had graduated from secondary school but did not make it into college. He was at the time stuck in military service, not sure what he was going to do with his life. His habit of smoking marijuana had caught up with him. God knows how much he broke my mom's heart over the years. At every opportunity, I would encourage my young brother to continue to pray for our elder brother as we would relax over a game of chess. Playing chess with me was one thing he would look forward to every time I would go home for the holidays. What I did not realize was that he had been practicing and had become quite good, such that he was able to beat me. I marveled at his determination but encouraged him to stay focused on school.

When I got back to school to start my fifth year in 1980, there was a sense of relief that permeated my life. Graduating from secondary school would soon be a reality. I was also apprehensive about the future and was not quite sure what I wanted to do, but I kept reminding myself to live in the moment and stay focused. I continued to participate in lots of extracurricular activities, including my responsibilities as a prefect. All things considered, I still found the time to study, especially late at night, as I had my own room and did not have to worry about distracting anyone. I was top of the class at the end of the first trimester. Nothing of significance really happened during that first trimester. I attended SU camp, which was held right at my school. It was a pleasure for us to host SU camp, as we got the chance to showcase our school to our hosts.

At the end of the second semester, instead of going home for the holidays or attending SU camp, I opted to help with the 1980 population census, which lasted a whole month. What made it interesting was that there was a stipend associated with this initiative. Besides, it was a great opportunity to make friends of the opposite sex, as there were volunteers from all the local schools.

During the first week, all participants had to attend training classes covering all the basics of how to fill out the forms, what to do when someone was not home, what to do when folks did not want to be counted, and so on. Classes ran from morning until about 2:00 to 3:00 p.m. One of the key benefits we discovered was that we were assigned a driver to take us where we needed to go as part of the census exercise. Seeing that we had the extra time in the afternoon, a fellow enumerator persuaded the driver to take us for a jolly ride. The driver had no objection, so a group of us boys and girls jumped in the van. That afternoon, we ended up at the river several miles from the Victoria Falls; it was the perfect campsite.

As we got out of the van, one of the girls whom I had never seen before caught my attention. I asked one of the other girls I was more comfortable with who she was. She indicated that the girl in question was her friend who had attended high school in Lusaka. However, her parents lived in Livingstone. She was home, having graduated from high school the prior year, and was waiting to enter the university that same year in September. I persuaded her to introduce me to her friend, and she gladly did. I was impressed to note that she was very friendly; her poise and self-confidence were unparalleled, but to my surprise, she was not very proud of her African name, Munalula. Her intelligence was simply impressive, and her sense of humor, quite wicked. She spoke English fluently; I was intimidated. Surprisingly, we became very good friends from the onset. She subsequently introduced me to her younger sister, who was equally charming.

Following the training, we embarked on the census for three consecutive weeks. Every morning, we would gather for a debriefing prior to going out in the field. On the first day, I was hoping I would be paired with the girl from Lusaka, but that wish never materialized. I was paired with another girl with whom I got along well but we shared no chemistry. However, we found a few moments of laughter and relaxation around lunch meals. Covering the entire assigned territory proved to be quite a challenge but, at the end of the three-week period, we had completed our tasks without too many obstacles. I had earlier hoped that the census would finish sooner in the hope of having the time to go home for at least a week. Not going home would have meant not being able to see my family until after the six-month period following national service, which was the next stage after high school. I dreaded the idea, and so I asked for permission to miss one week of school. The deputy headmaster understood my dilemma and allowed me to go home. I took my visit and returned to school for the final stretch.

The trimester I had looked forward to finally arrived. It did not take me long to catch up on the one week I had missed; I slowly began to give up my responsibilities in extracurricular engagements. New prefects were also appointed, but we did not lose our privileges. We did what we could to support the new group of prefects, but our time had come and gone. We were lame ducks in the interim. The focus was entirely on the looming exams. I was a slow writer generally, so I focused on training myself to write fast in readiness for the one and half hours long history exam. One had to pick three essay topics out of thirty. I trained myself to eyeball all the thirty essay topics in just under three minutes and then compose the first essay in about twenty-seven to twenty-eight minutes. I got to the point where I could write seven to eight pages in this time frame.

During the previous mock exams, I had not done very well in physics. In preparation, I studied the physics textbook twice, back to back. I did not care much about my grade in metalwork; the three-hour practical exam was probably a lost case for most of us. I did not need much preparation in the two mathematics subjects I was taking, and I was okay in chemistry, but still needed to brush up on several topics. Not much study was required in technical drawing; all I needed was additional practice in conceptualizing mechanical objects in space when they are sectioned. No additional effort was required in English, but I reviewed a few past English papers just to ensure I was comfortable with the format. That was the strategy going into the final stretch. As my grade school teacher taught us, it was about leaving no stone unturned. I was somewhat apprehensive, but my focus was intense.

We started our exams around the middle of November. This time around, we had a few days in between successive exams. The night before each exam, we gathered as brothers in Christ and laid our hands on one another, praying fervently for God's will to be done, and then we wished one another success. The first exam was practical metalwork, followed by practical chemistry, and then physics. After the practical exams, we moved into the exam hall for the duration of the exam period. The last exam for me was additional mathematics. I was already exhausted by then but ploughed through to the best of my ability. When it was all over, what a sigh of relief it was for everyone! We had graduated from secondary school. I looked for my brothers in Christ, and we all retired to a secluded place to praise our God. We sang, cried, and prayed together for more than an hour. The outpouring we experienced was never to be forgotten; we all knew this was the last time we would ever be together under similar settings.

On December 5, we boarded the train going to Lusaka, where we would be picked up and distributed to the various military camps throughout the country. One journey had ended, and another was about to start. As the train left the platform, we bade farewell to the city that had seen us grow from boys to men. We left behind beautiful memories of the Victoria Falls, our teachers, our beloved school, and most importantly, the five years we had spent trying to mold our lives into something better. Only time would tell what the future would portend.

Fig 5: One of the seven wonders of the natural world; the Victoria Falls in Livingstone where I spent my secondary school years

Fig 6: The Presbyterian church I used to attend during my secondary school years in Livingstone

Figure 7: My fourth year in Secondary School

Fig 8: Sharing a moment with fellow census participants during the 1980 census. Who would have known that one of the ladies in the picture would become Zambia's first lady?

CHAPTER 5

National Service, College, and Transition into the Next World

Military service was at the time mandatory for all students graduating from high school. There were several reasons the government instituted national service. Firstly, the volatile situation in a neighboring country, Southern Rhodesia, where the war for independence was still in progress, constituted a viable threat to the nation. Secondly, students graduating from high school were spending almost nine months out of school prior to starting college. The concern was that they were contributing to the increase in the crime rate and other juvenile vices. Therefore, in the politicians' eyes, sending them to military camps was a national service imperative and a step in the right direction.

We arrived in Lusaka the following morning and were commanded to sit down and wait for instructions by one of the low-ranking army officers. After waiting for more than an hour, I got up to stretch my legs.

The low-ranking officer immediately charged toward me and slapped me. "Did I not tell you all to sit down and wait for my instructions?" he asked.

I attempted to say something in response, but the guy gave me no chance. That was a foretaste of the abuse we would endure for the following six months, at minimum.

Later, we were told that our group would be heading to the camp in Ndola. We boarded the train in the evening and reached our destination the following morning, where military trucks were all around, waiting to take us to camp in the designated towns. By the time we got to camp, we were very tired and hungry, but our day was just beginning. After everyone had arrived, the camp commander gave a short speech, welcoming us to the campsite. The essence of his speech was that he was looking forward to breaking us down and later building us into new men. It sounded like a well-crafted joke at the time, but little did we know that he meant it. He then handed over the mundane tasks to the lower-ranking officers. The first order of business was to assign us to our various companies and platoons. We were each given one set of military uniforms and a pair of exercise gear and then asked to surrender all our casual clothes. We were then shown to our barracks, which were to be our homes for the duration of the six-month period. After an unpalatable dinner (consisting of nshima and several grains of beans in colored water), we retired to our barracks and attempted to rest. Just a few nights prior, I had been sleeping in the comfort of my own room at school, but now I found myself in unfamiliar territory. The truth, however, was that I could not have a better tomorrow if I kept thinking about my yesterday. It was time to embrace this experience as another stepping-stone into the future.

We were awakened the following day at 4:00 a.m. by the attending sergeants and asked to line up in single file by platoon. On his orders, we started jogging, heading out of the camp. Singing and chanting, as we were about to learn, was a big part of a recruit's life. In a group setting, this could be quite a morale booster. The attending staff immediately started teaching us a few songs and chants as we accelerated our pace. The chants were such that he would shout a phrase and then expect us to respond in harmony.

Before we even knew it, we had run more than ten kilometers and were headed back to camp, as were the other companies. The sound of recruits from different companies all singing or chanting was music to the ear. Following morning exercise, we were treated to breakfast, which consisted of a slice of bread and a cup of tea. What was excruciatingly painful was the time we had to spend queuing; it took quite a while to feed about two thousand recruits. Unfortunately, if it was time for the next activity and you were still in line, it was time to forfeit the meal. After breakfast, we took quick showers and then headed for the morning parade of the entire battalion. This was the time the officers used to conduct a general inspection to ensure that all recruits were properly attired. Those who were found lacking in any way were subjected to some form of punishment, including but not limited to missing meals. The camp commander would then make any announcements of relevance. Following the morning parade, we would break up into our companies and begin with the program for the day. On our second day in camp, all those with long hair were taken to the barbershop, and had their heads shaved to the bone.

Learning to march was what we spent a lot of time on during the first week. We also attended classes and received instruction on topics related to citizenry and general behavior. As well intentioned as the classes were, unfortunately, the instructors were not competent. The real program began in the second week when each one of us was handed a rifle with the caution that the rifle was a wife we could not afford to lose. For the following two weeks, we practiced how to disassemble and assemble a rifle until we were able to do it in practically minutes. At the end of the six-month training program, there was a prize awarded to the recruit who could do it in the shortest time possible.

As time went by, we started getting used to the routines of military life. Wherever you were, when an officer passed by, you were supposed to stop and salute him. You did not move until he gave you permission to move on. Officers had the right to punish us as they saw fit, sometimes for very minor infractions. One form of punishment I really detested was a spontaneous soak. When the order was given, you had no time to empty your pockets; you were submerged as you were without hesitation. For more severe infractions, such as being AWOL (away without official leave), there was a special place called the guard room. The guard room was basically a prison; it was the worst place in camp you could ever dream of wanting to be. I was lucky enough not to ever find myself there, but other recruits or cadets who had been sent there described the inhumane conditions.

To move from point A to point B, we had to go marching. If we were in a group, we would form a single line, and one person in the group would lead the march. Morning exercises were tough, but after some time, we began to appreciate how strong we were becoming. I recall we used to lift heavy logs from different positions in lieu of dumbbells.

Our biggest problem in camp was hunger. The quality of the food was very bad. Unfortunately, the issue was not merely the quality; the portions were so small that, given the level of training we were subjected to, we were always hungry. We started stealing corn (maize cobs), sweet potatoes, cassava, and other produce from nearby farms. It was not long before the owners lodged complaints with the camp commander, who took measures to curb the behavior.

After about a month in camp, we had the first opportunity to go to the gun range. This was an exercise that we all enjoyed. We were each given a total of ten bullets and asked to shoot at stationary targets placed at a distance of about two hundred yards. As I recall, I probably hit the target 50 percent of the time, which was considered not good enough. My forte was actually map reading; in this exercise, we were driven out of camp, left in the middle of the jungle, and then asked to find our way back to the camp using only a compass and a map. Not only were we expected to find our way back to camp, but we were also expected to pick up certain objects that had been left along the way. If you arrived at camp after dinner, you had to fend for yourself, and there was nothing you could do about that. On our first try, I volunteered to be the leader of our platoon. Our group was the first to arrive at camp, having picked up all the assigned objects on the way, to the delight of the folks in my group. On two other occasions, when we repeated this exercise, I led my team to victory and therefore earned the honor of best map reader at graduation.

Those of us who identified ourselves as Christians organized and started having regular worship meetings in the evening, after dinner. When others became aware of the meetings, attendance increased so much that we ran out of room. We used to take turns preaching.

Whenever we learned that a brother in Christ had a special need, we found ways to help as a group in addition to prayer. We forged strong bonds of camaraderie and friendship for the duration of the six-month period. Occasionally, we would invite guest speakers to address the group. This was what kept us going; despite the tough camp conditions, we found a way to alleviate the load by being there for one another and focusing on our faith.

Form 5 results were usually announced around the March–April time frame. As the day drew closer, we started getting anxious. For most of us, it was not clear how we would learn about our results, considering we were in a remote camp, separated from human civilization. I was coming out of the dining hall one evening when I approached a group of guys from my school, talking excitedly. In the middle of that conversation, I heard my name mentioned, and that caught my attention. It turned out that one of the colleagues from our school had received a letter from a friend, the contents of which included the results of some notable names. There were no details, just a summary of the total points earned by the top three to five students. This time, I was not on top.

Within a few days, we found a way to have the detailed results communicated to us. I had scored five As, two Bs, and a C. These results were good enough to earn a place at any university of my choice. What I had been hoping for was a scholarship with the mining company. The mines had very good scholarship programs to the UK, but in our intake, they decided to suspend the issuance of scholarships temporarily. The only opportunity for scholarships available at the time was for the Accounting program. I decided to try for these scholarships, even though I was not sure I had an interest in accounting.

Before completing our six-month military training, we had to survive the war games. This was the climax of the program; we had heard stories from previous attendees that some recruits had died going through this program. We were driven to an unknown location late at night and dropped off in the middle of a thick jungle. From there, we started walking, not knowing where we were going. You simply followed the person in front of you. We must have walked for about six hours nonstop, arriving at the site for the war games at approximately 3:00 a.m. As soon as we arrived, an order was given for us to start digging trenches, where we were expected to take cover in the face of enemy fire. Halfway through the process, the enemy company descended upon us, firing blanks. We took cover in our trenches and fired back. If you were not in the trenches, you were captured as a prisoner of war (POW). The digging and fighting went on until dawn; at that point, we were quite exhausted. To make matters worse, it started raining so heavily that our trenches were soaked. Under this scenario, there really was nowhere to hide. We could not make a fire to cook something warm, and we felt miserable under these circumstances, which we endured for about three days. I have no idea how we survived such unbearable conditions. Finally, the order was given to start walking back to camp. This time, there was no transportation of any kind. We walked all the way to the camp, and it probably took us half a day. Each time we passed nearby farmed areas, we ransacked almost anything that was in our way. As we approached the camp, we broke into singing and chanting. As hungry and tired as we were, we had not lost our motivation. We ate dinner that evening and retired to bed almost immediately since there were no planned adjustments for the following day's schedule. We still had to wake up at 4:00 a.m.

Following the war games, a sense of optimism permeated the camp. It became apparent that graduation day was in sight. Almost daily, time was allocated for the rehearsals associated with graduation day. We would practice marching drills over and over until the instructors were satisfied that we would not mess up on graduation day. Those of us due to receive certificates of recognition rehearsed in front of the entire battalion how to break from the ranks when called upon and march to the improvised dais. On many occasions, I was soaked in water for either making the wrong turn or turning too slowly. By the time the month of June rolled around, the mood in camp was much more relaxed; we had more time for leisure, and there were days we would just hang out and chill because there was nothing else to do. The day prior to graduation, I received a notification to attend interviews with the mines in Chingola, scheduled two weeks after graduation. I was excited but not overly ecstatic. I made the decision, however, to attend the interviews, and I informed my friends about it.

Graduation day was our time to shine and showcase the skills we had acquired. The podium was filled with special dignitaries from Lusaka—politicians, high-ranking military officials, and family members who could afford to attend. We put up a good show, displaying our skills, including marching as a group while carrying our weapons. When I was called upon to receive my certificate as the best recruit in map reading, I acknowledged at the top of my voice, shouting, "Sir!" Then I raised my weapon shoulder-high, broke out of my rank, made several turns until I was in the open, and headed straight to the podium, marching rhythmically. I arrived at the podium, dropped my weapon, and saluted. When I got the salute back, I took a few steps forward and froze, looking up straight. If a bee had bitten me at that point, I would not have moved. Such was the discipline that had been instilled in our psyche. I was handed the certificate, which I received with my left hand, and then extended my right for a handshake. I took a few steps back, saluted, raised my weapon, and turned around as the audience broke into applause. I had done it!

The final act before official graduation was that of tossing our berets into the air. When the "Hep hep!" prompt was heard, we shouted "Hurray!" and tossed our berets in the air as far as we could. That concluded the graduation ceremony.

I left camp the following week on a Monday and headed home to visit my family. They were overjoyed to see me. A few days later, I travelled to my former school, where I needed to pick up my academic credentials. Arriving in Livingstone brought back so many beautiful memories; I lodged at the apartment of our SU patron, a British man. We found time to catch up on several issues. After several days, I was on my way back home with less than a week to prepare for the interviews with the mines. I proceeded to Chingola Accountancy College, where I was surprised to note that there were more than 200 students who had been invited for the interviews. Only 20 would make the final cut.

After the first round of interviews, which consisted of general knowledge questions, the list was trimmed to 120 candidates, then to 80, and subsequently, 40. The 40 candidates were then allowed to move forward to the face-to-face interviews before the panel. In the end, 20 of us were selected.

We started college classes almost immediately. The terms of our scholarships were simple; we would spend two years at the Accountancy Training College in Chingola and another two years in the UK. The scholarship included tuition, room and board, and books, as well as stationery. On top of that, we were paid a stipend of about $100 every two weeks. The campus was quite beautiful, with well-manicured lawns and spacious hostel rooms, which were shared between two students. Cleaning and laundry were taken care of by cleaning service workers; they practically did everything for us. If you had clothes to wash, you left them on the bed, and by the time you returned from class, everything would be nicely folded. Meals were quite decent. All we were asked to do was to show up, study, and pass the exams.

It was not long after we commenced classes that I made friends with a classmate called Dimas. He and I shared the same faith, and therefore, we started attending a local church together. There were other brothers and sisters in Christ on campus. We organized ourselves and started meeting for Bible study and prayer. On a few occasions, we invited external guest speakers. My new friend and I shared many beautiful moments. We were at that stage in our lives where finding a life partner was becoming a priority; we both had crushes on some girls in the church we attended. There was never a day when their names did not come up in conversation. Some of the brothers ahead of us had established relationships heading toward marriage, and this was an opportunity for us to learn from them.

We took our first exams in December. I performed well, but my result in accounting could have been better. We were then sent on internships to acquire practical skills as accountants in training. My assignment was in Kitwe, working at one of the electrical companies. I had a few challenges with work colleagues who had been working there as junior accountants because they were asked to start reporting to me as supervisor. The corner office they had craved for so long was now mine. They did not like it a bit and did not hide their disgust that a kid from college was going to be their boss. I understood and did my best to win their trust, but only time would tell. One of the senior accountants working in the office used to take me on assignments to client companies. The experience of getting out of the office was quite refreshing given the antagonism I faced almost every day with the three subordinate junior accountants. I was, at the time, sharing a house with a colleague of mine who had just separated from his wife.

Time kept ticking, and we were not called back to the college to continue our program. I became desperate; from where I stood, this was not what I had signed up for. I had thought we would complete the two-year program in one straight shot. My doubts created anxiety, which led to frustration. Before long, I had decided it was time to quit. The only problem was, if I was going to go to the university, I would have to wait until September for the next intake. I even took time off and travelled to the capital city, Lusaka, to enquire about the possibility of enrolling and also to consult some friends who were, at the time, completing their first year at the University of Zambia. This was a period of confusion for me because I had no clarity as to what my future portended.

Reading the newspaper one weekend, I saw an advertisement for scholarships to Cuba. I applied without hesitation and was pleasantly surprised to be called for an interview almost right away. I returned to Lusaka to attend the interview, which was not an interview as such, but just an opportunity to hear more about the program. I was handed a few forms, one of which was an application for a passport. From Lusaka, I travelled to my parents' home. When I arrived, one of the girls I used to attend church with, Mary, was visiting my mom. Our mothers were very good friends, and so I was not surprised to find her there. I immediately asked her if she could submit the passport forms on my behalf, and she agreed without hesitation, on the condition that I provided money for transportation. We spent the rest of that evening filling out the forms. There was an affidavit of oath that needed to be signed by someone close to the family. My mom recommended asking the reverend at our local church, who was more than happy to help; it most certainly took a village to raise a kid in our community. Two days later, Mary travelled to the passport office in Ndola. In the evening, I decided to wait for her at the bus station. As soon as she stepped out of the bus and saw me, she handed me the passport and mumbled something to the effect that she had played a small role in my life and would appreciate if I would remember that. I hugged her spontaneously, telling her what a great friend she was.

I still had doubts about whether it made sense to leave for Cuba or not. At this point in my life, I had come to realize that God was not only a Master Strategist but also a Master Tactician. When He deals with us, He always begins with the end in mind. I had on previous occasions seen what He could do. I just needed to trust Him more. Armed with faith and resolution, I tendered my resignation and started preparing for the trip to Cuba.

It was not long thereafter that my mom suffered a stroke while in Kitwe, attending a women's church conference. She was rushed to the Kitwe Central Hospital, where the doctors determined that she had to be confined for some time. One of the nurses attending to her turned out to be the girlfriend of one of my college mates. She promised to keep me informed on her condition as time went by. Prior to leaving for Lusaka, where I had a host of issues to attend to related to the Cuba scholarship, I travelled to the hospital to see my mom, picking up a box of ice cream on my way. Upon arrival, it dawned on me that her condition was probably worse than I had previously thought; she looked frail and could hardly talk. When our eyes met, I put up a brave face and forced a smile. She smiled in return. Deep inside, I was devastated. I pointed to the ice cream and asked if she was ready to have some.

"Perhaps later," she replied.

I held her hand and assured her that she was going to be all right, as she looked at me skeptically. I then changed the topic and let her know that I had made the decision to take the scholarship to Cuba. She did not know how to react but encouraged me to go. It was in that moment that I let her know that I was not going to have another chance to see her before my departure. She was obviously in pain, but she tried leaning forward to give me a hug. It was the last hug I would receive from my mother for quite some time. I left quickly, trying to avoid an imminent emotional breakdown that threatened to engulf both of us.

The journey into my next life was about to begin. I arrived in Lusaka and attended to immediate needs related to the scholarship, to give myself time to bid farewell to my friends at the University of Zambia. Out of sheer coincidence, and very fortunately, I ran into Munalula, the girl who had captured my attention during the census. We had stayed in touch since then, and I always looked forward to receiving her letters, which were sweet to read. She had been awarded a scholarship to study medicine in one of the Eastern European countries shortly after the census. She was on vacation at the time. It was a joyous moment for both of us as we found time to catch up. When I informed her that I was getting ready to go to Cuba, she really encouraged me to take a bold step and trust God completely. That was all the assurance I needed. Two days later, I ran into Glenda, the girl who had been to my house previously. She was very happy for me and assured me of her prayers every day. I then reached out to my friends at the University of Zambia who were now just about to finish their first year, and they were very gracious to the point of spending time with me in prayer.

The time had come for me to leave my beloved Zambia. I was encouraged to note that there were a few students from my former secondary school who would be traveling with me. It was quite a venture into the unknown, but I had resolved in my heart of hearts that my God would still be my guide. As we boarded the flight to Kenya, my mind raced through an array of confusing and conflicting thoughts. If there was any consolation or lesson for me to grasp, it was that I had seen what God could do, and there was no doubt that He was merely laying the foundation for what was to come. All I asked God for was the opportunity to be able to see my ailing mother again, and God, who is so rich in mercy, surely heard my prayer and would prove Himself faithful again and again, but not until He had brought me to the point of teaching me patience and complete surrender to His will. I then understood what Martin Luther, a patriarch of the Christian faith, meant when he wrote, "The just shall live by faith."

PART 2

The Island

CHAPTER 6
Reflections: First Impressions

Following several layovers along the way, with one in London and
the other in Canada, we arrived in Cuba several hours past midnight.
Exhausted and sleepy, we went through the immigration formalities. Our escort from the Ministry of Education identified himself
to the Cuban authorities, and after exchanging pleasantries, we were
whisked to a private room for a headcount and further instructions.
It was at that point that we became aware that our checked luggage
had gone missing, which further delayed checkout procedures at the
airport, as we had to file missing luggage reports. It was probably close
to 4:00 a.m. when we finally boarded the bus that was to take us to
an undisclosed location somewhere on the outskirts of Havana. We
would later learn that our destination was the Tropical Quarantine
Hospital, where we would be screened for tropical illnesses prior to
being allowed to interact with the Cuban people.

In terms of first impressions, several things stood out in my mind
as we drove through the streets of Havana. First, having been acclima-
tized to the low Zambian humidity, I found the humid heat in Cuba
suffocating; it would take me a long time to get used to this specific
aspect of the island's weather. The lack of air-conditioning on the bus
made the situation even more unbearable, as we were all sweating pro-
fusely. Secondly, I noticed a plethora of billboards with political slogans
all along the way, mostly directed at the Imperialist Yankees. I would
later learn who the Yankees were and their place in the history of the
island nation. Perhaps the most striking of all my early impressions was
what I perceived to be underdevelopment of the infrastructure along

91

the way. The city looked like a war zone and exuded a smell that was extraordinary. As I gathered my thoughts during the ride to the quarantine hospital, I started to entertain misgivings about my decision to come to Cuba. I felt demoralized, as if the wind had been sucked out of my lungs, but there was no turning back. I reminded myself of several comforting passages in scripture, subsequently immersing my thoughts in the peace that surpasses all understanding.

We arrived at the quarantine hospital at the break of dawn with eleven other Zambian colleagues. The other group of twenty-three Zambians was directed to another quarantine location. My anxiety returned upon arrival at what looked like a makeshift hospital. Living conditions were not the best; there were bunk beds sprawled across a large room, where students from many parts of Africa, the Caribbean, and the Americas were quarantined. There was no privacy whatsoever. Toilet facilities were few and certainly not sufficient to accommodate all the students comfortably. Trying to sleep under such conditions was next to impossible. There were a few chairs on the tiny patio, and it was not surprising that no one was willing to give those up once secured early in the morning. The only other option was to stay in bed the whole day. There was no TV to watch or any other form of entertainment. The nurses would go around, dispensing medications, which we were required to take, no questions asked. I recall feeling drowsy and nauseated as a side effect from the medication.

We were at this point identified as the Zambia *doce*, simply translated to mean the Zambian group of twelve. When it was time for medications or meals, the nurse would shout "Zambia doce!" and expect us to identify ourselves in response. We were not even asked if we had any form of allergies to certain types of medication. In a sense, it felt like a military camp. Seven days of quarantine with no exercise whatsoever seemed like an eternity. My first experience of a Cuban meal was quite disappointing. For a start, I was disgusted with the serving plates known as *bandejas* in Spanish. These were like the type we had used when I underwent military service back in Zambia. One dish, I recall, was fried plantains. The food looked and smelled so bad that I do not know how I managed to consume it. Flies were all over the place, and it just felt like I had gone back in time. On the third morning, I woke up early out of desperation, went to the patio, knelt, and began to pray. I was not even aware that I was attracting attention, as my desperation level at this point was at its peak. Without knowing, one of the nurses saw me praying and looked at me in utter disbelief as if she had never in her life seen anyone pray.

It was quite an experience, starting life in Cuba on such a low note. Every single foreign student who passed through that hospital only had a negative reaction to the circumstances they had endured. In retrospect, we were all left to wonder why the Cuban government would choose this locale as a "first-impressions-welcoming" experience. The seven days went by very slowly.

After what seemed like an eternity, we were declared to have met the minimum health requirements to be able to integrate into Cuban society. A bus from the Ministry of Education picked us up and drove us to what was going to be our language school for the academic year starting in September of 1982. The school was located on the outskirts of the Greater Havana region, probably about an hour's drive from the quarantine hospital. As we were transported to our destination, we had the opportunity to see parts of the city up close and in broad daylight for the first time. The architectural structures caught my attention; the edifices looked old and dilapidated, mostly Spanish constructions in need of serious paint jobs. Some of the old buildings looked like they would collapse if not given immediate attention. Most of the cars on the street were old American-made models from the early 1950s. The latest cars on the road consisted of simple Lada models, which I understood later were a Soviet Union brand. It was as if we had stepped into the past! Could I have expected anything fancier from a satellite of the Eastern bloc?

We drove past several schools and saw happy kids going about their usual business without too much fanfare. There were a few moments along the way of sheer ecstasy when we would see a beautiful mulata "criolla" (Cuban-born) woman scantily dressed, with a well-rounded rear attracting catcalls from near and far. We would look at each other approvingly. One of the comrades in the group retorted instantly that he could not wait to learn Spanish, triggering nods from everyone. That was wishful thinking by comrade Mumba, a gifted comedian by every stretch of the imagination. If there was such a thing as a demeanor default setting, there was no doubt that his could be characterized as perpetual joy. I would learn later that in Cuban colloquial or street language, the well-rounded phenomenon was dubbed "tinajon" in Camaguey (one of the provinces on the island) and there was no shortage of this desirable feature in Cuban women, wherever the roving eye fell. All major races, I observed, were well represented in Cuban society. Given the history of the Spanish conquest, the slave trade and the economy of the sugar plantations, the confluence of the races was more than palpable.

Before long, we had reached our destination. The language school was in an isolated farming community, and so the hustles and bustles of city life were totally absent. The location of the school in this community was probably intended to focus students away from the distractions of city life in direct proximity with Cubans. The school was a four-story building, with classrooms, an assembly hall, staff facilities, a play area, and dining facilities on the first and second floors. Dormitories were located on the third and fourth floors; each dormitory had its own toilet and shower facilities.

School was not scheduled to start for about a month, and therefore there was plenty of time to relax and acclimatize. We went through the formalities of checking in and being shown our dormitories by someone from the Ministry of Education who spoke understandable English. Eight of us were confined to one of the dormitories with four bunk beds (or *literas* as they were commonly known). The other four Zambian students shared a dormitory with students from other countries. We met students from African countries such as Ghana, Angola, Mozambique, and Zimbabwe to name but a few. The Americas were also represented in the melting pot, including Suriname, Guyana, and Belize. We even had students from as far away as Palestine, Mongolia, and Cambodia. Most of the students spoke English, which facilitated our communication experience. Meals were served three times a day; the quality of the meals was acceptable. Before long, I had developed a craving for yoghurt as it was commonly served with every meal. Except for the constantly buzzing flies during meals, and mosquitos that made it impossible to sleep at night, we were slowly beginning to adapt to this strange environment we would call home for the duration of the first year.

Our first order of business was to find our way to the city to buy a few much-needed clothes, considering our luggage had been misrouted while in transit. We inquired from other students who had been there longer on how to get to the city. Based on their advice, we had to pick a combination of two bus routes to get to Coppelia (a popular ice-cream parlor and gateway to downtown Havana), which was within walking distance of the Havana Libre Hotel and other places of interest. As instructed, we boarded the first bus to La Lisa, and from there another to Coppelia. The experience of riding on the bus for the first time was quite a thrill. My first observation of interest was that the bus fare was only five cents to any part of the city. As newbies, we did not have pesos (Cuban currency). Noticing that we were new and could not communicate in Spanish, the bus driver signaled to us to get on board without paying and so did the next driver on the second leg of the trip. "If this is what fraternity is in a socialist society, then maybe it's worth taking a second look," I thought to myself as we rode to our destination.

Local buses were often crowded beyond the recommended maximum occupancy standards, but no one really complained about the overcrowding. My observation was that some of the male passengers relished the idea of crowded buses, as this condition facilitated proximity with members of the opposite sex and therefore unsolicited touching was free for the taking without being easily noticed.

Arriving at Coppelia, we disembarked without a clue of where to head. Our immediate goal was to exchange dollars into the local currency, and to buy some clothes. As we walked past Hotel Havana Libre in the direction of Malecon, a taxi sped by and stopped a short distance ahead. A "curvilicious" blond woman stepped out and raced in front of us, swinging her hips from side to side. We admired from a distance, unaware that she was courting our attention. A few minutes later, the same taxi (bearing the rear number plate) that had dropped her off picked her up and raced off. We looked at one another in disbelief as we attempted to digest the meaning of that experience. It smelled like broad daylight prostitution from where I stood.

We stopped at the bank and asked to change dollars into Cuban pesos. The lady at the counter proceeded to assist us with the transaction, suggesting in addition that there was a shop exclusively for foreigners in Havana Libre Hotel across the street. We learned afterward that foreigners in Cuba had special shops where Cubans were not allowed to go. These shops were known as *diplo-tiendas*. Merchandise in these shops was sold exclusively in foreign currencies. We became aware rather quickly that exchange of foreign currencies on the black market was a well-established underground enterprise. We lamented having exchanged some of our money at the bank, where the Peso was rated higher than the dollar. Worse still, we discovered to our dismay that we could not buy clothes with the Cuban pesos for reasons we never understood at the time. Having picked up a few necessities from the dollar shop in Havana Libre hotel and later some ice cream at Coppelia, we returned to school just in time for dinner.

For the next few weeks, we would spend much of the time becoming acclimated to our new environment. There wasn't much to do other than get to know our schoolmates from other countries and exchange information about our respective homelands. On the second floor of the building, there was a black and white TV that kept us entertained. We also played ping-pong as well as chess to dispel the boredom, in addition to taking the opportunity to write letters to family and friends. Thinking that I might get good advice about the socialist system, I also wrote to Munalula, who was studying in Eastern Europe at the time. My motivation was to learn about the socialist system from her experience. She was gracious enough to recount her experiences in response. Hearing from her was a breath of fresh air, not to mention the fact that I had harbored a crush on her during my high school days and still held the hope of a more perfect union in the future.

One experience of interest during this period was meeting a student from Ghana who would turn out to be one of my closest friends in Cuba. Kofi just came wandering into our dorm one day, bored to death like everyone else. After introducing himself, he asked if there were any Christians in our group, to which I responded in the affirmative. He smiled cheerfully and gave me a big handshake. That handshake was the beginning of a great friendship, hooked up in heaven from the get-go. As an individual, Kofi had a great personality. Unlike me, he was an extrovert, a go-getter. I grasped that he had the capacity to interact with almost anyone; people who met him were instantly attracted to him. He was confident, persuasive, and a great charmer. He was bold, spoke his mind freely, and was articulate in most topics of interest. Women who got to know him found him irresistible. Unfortunately, his strengths were also his weaknesses. Too often I noticed what an arrogant and self-centered individual he could be.

As we chatted for the first time, he indicated that he was a member of the Seventh Day Adventist Church (SDA) and that, prior to going to Cuba, he had researched the various locations in the greater Havana area for SDA churches. Several days after, he invited me to go with him in search of the closest church address he had. I had no reason to object, even though I was not a member of his faith, as such. We found the church without too much effort, given that Cubans were very helpful to foreigners in general despite the language barrier.

The SDA church in Marianao turned out to be quite vibrant despite my preconceived notions of religious suppression in a socialist society. The entire church was very welcoming to us as two foreign students among the parishioners. After the evening service, we found ourselves surrounded by a host of young men and women who wanted to chat with us. Despite the language barrier, we really felt welcome and started attending church services regularly. Every Sabbath, we would be invited for lunch at a different home. I began to appreciate just how faithful members of the SDA church were in observing the Sabbath as a period of rest and worship from Friday evening to Saturday evening. As such, they would prepare all their meals prior to the Sabbath. This was certainly not something I was accustomed to in my practice of Christianity and it took some getting used to.

There were two families we were introduced to that we developed a special affinity for; one was a family of Jamaican descent who spoke English quite fluently. We got to learn with the lapse of time that they had family in the US. The other was a black Cuban family that lived on a farm not too far from where our school was located. There were two girls in this family within our age group, both of whom were single. Before long, we had become good friends. They helped us get a head start with our Spanish. It was not long thereafter that the older of the two developed a crush on my friend Kofi. He knew she liked him, but he gave her a hard time by pretending that he was not interested. Her frustration was palpable. We would visit their farm occasionally and their mother would prepare sumptuous meals for us. At the end of each visit, the girls would walk us to the bus station, a few blocks from their home. We grew to cherish their company and friendship over time.

CHAPTER 7
Language School

The time had come for us to start our Spanish classes. Preparation school was not exclusively about learning Spanish. It was also meant to provide remedial classes to ensure students were well prepared upon entry in the university. Taking technical classes also provided the opportunity to familiarize ourselves with the technical language in Spanish. Given the background I had in high school, the remedial classes for me were a breeze; the only thing I needed to focus on was Spanish. On our first day, we got to meet our Spanish instructor, who was short and stout with a great sense of humor. Overall, she was a good teacher and it was obvious that she was really interested in our concerns beyond the classroom as well. She also felt that it was her obligation to inform us of the various places of interest to visit, in addition to the arts and social activities going on around the city. We followed her advice, and quickly discovered how beautiful and friendly the country and its people were. One piece of advice she kept repeating over and over was that the only way we were going to learn Spanish was to go out there and hook up with Cuban girls. She herself was dating a foreign student from one of the Caribbean islands who was at the time studying at one of the local universities. By her own confession, her boyfriend was a former student at the same language school where she taught.

Not long after we had started our classes, Kofi and I were invited to lunch after church service at the home of one of the members. As usual, we were treated to a very delicious meal. Following lunch, the man of the house brought to our attention the fact that he had received some money from his family in the US through someone who was visiting from Miami. He requested that we take him to the diplo-tiendas to spend it. Being new in Cuba, we did not think much of it and obliged without raising any concerns, arranging to meet that same evening after sunset. We went to several shops in a few of the hotels. My friend did much of the purchasing; I was just there in a supportive role. Prior to heading to the Riviera Hotel, the Cubans left us to carry some of the merchandise home and agreed to meet us later at the Riviera Hotel. It turned out to be a blessing in disguise that our Cuban friends left at the time they did.

As we looked around for additional merchandise, we were approached by state security personnel, who asked us to follow them. We were not quite sure what had ensued as we were led through a series of corridors to a waiting police car. It then dawned on us that we were being arrested. Without any explanation, we were detained and booked at the nearest detention center to the hotel. Our inability to express ourselves well in Spanish coupled with our naiveté made it even more challenging as we could not adequately assimilate or convey what had just happened. Summarily, the charges were that we had conspired to illegally engage in buying and selling merchandise to Cubans. We were kept at the detention center for almost four days and three nights.

Meanwhile, my colleagues at school had no idea what happened to me. They reported the issue to the language school director, who had been briefed about the incident behind the scenes but pretended not to know anything. He did, however, promise my Zambian schoolmates that he was going to look into the issue. Maintaining a code of silence about so called "state secrets" was the norm in Cuban society and rather telling of how much control the state exercised even on the most mundane of issues. On the fourth day, a representative from the Ministry of Education came to talk to us, primarily wanting to know what had happened. To the best of my ability, I tried to communicate my confusion about the arrest and how I did not think we had done anything illegal other than try to buy merchandise from the dollar store. My friend Kofi, on the other hand, who was by no means a pacifist like me, was arguing that this incident constituted a violation of our rights under international law, questioning the stance of the Cuban government on human rights. Taking note of the rigorous defense he was mounting and certainly not wishing to see escalation of the issue into an international crisis, the authorities released us without charging us and asked us to return to school.

Rather than head to school, we opted to first visit the Jamaican family we knew from Church, as they had become our most trusted confidants. They did their best to bring to our attention the common abuses so prevalent in the socialist state. People were arrested for all sorts of petty offenses, such as attempting to sell personal belongings to their neighbors if they had extras. Later, we returned to school and joined the regular activities without much fanfare. My Spanish instructor was relieved to see me but did not say much other than "Welcome back, vacationist," to which I responded, "Thank you very much." While this occurrence was isolated and quickly forgotten with the passing of time, it made me realize very early on that the freedoms I took for granted while growing up in my society were unfortunately not universal.

It was worth noting that the Cuban national hero Jose Marti was quoted extensively in most of the materials related to our Spanish classes to convey not only his literary prowess but also his philosophy and love for the homeland. As I started to read and write Spanish, I quickly became aware that his writings were quite profound and demonstrated a remarkable spirit of patriotism. One day, our Spanish teacher asked us to write an essay on a specific topic related to the writings of Jose Marti. I did some research on the subject and wrote a two-page summary of what I understood to be the central theme. The Spanish instructor was so impressed with my work that she took the time to read the essay in front of the entire class. Not only did she do that, but she also went a step further and brought the paper to the attention of the dean. As a result of her meeting with the dean, she then asked me to read the essay in front of everyone in the school. From that point on, things were never quite the same again between us; I had won her trust and respect and could never do anything wrong. Sensing this, I took it as the opportune moment to let her know that I had a religious background and would always strive to remain true to my Christian values. I do not think she was particularly impressed with this confession, but at least she understood where I was coming from.

My other teachers turned out to be nice and easygoing. The physics instructor, for one, was by every measure a great man that was well liked by everyone. He came across as one who had reservations about his political beliefs, which he kept to himself. Inside and outside the classroom, he discussed nothing but physics. The chemistry teacher was a young woman who had studied in the Soviet Union. She was a sociable personality, who was always smiling, communicative, and outgoing; I got the sense that she was stuck in a system that she was not very happy about but did her best to go with the flow. Maybe that explained her addiction to smoking. Then there was the math teacher, who would never stop talking. He was quite charming in conversation, but math had always been my favorite subject since high school, so I took it upon myself to correct him whenever he veered off course. For that reason, he had great respect for me and never bothered me.

I never quite understood how the Cuban system of rationing goods was structured until I decided one day to go and buy an electrical fan that I had seen at one of the Cuban shops. I told the shopkeeper that I was interested in purchasing the displayed item. He simply waved a finger in front of me, uttering, "Solo con tarjeta." (Only with a ration card.) I was a little confused, but it became clear that even though I had the money, I could not complete the purchase. Upon returning to school, a colleague from Uganda who was repeating language school was kind enough to walk me through the details.

While I never quite understood all the intricacies of the rationing system, the economic embargo on Cuba by successive US administrations made it necessary to ration food in a well-meaning attempt to ensure every individual had a supply of basics for sustenance. Families were assigned a given quantity of rice, meat, and flour based on the number of individuals in a family unit. If a family ran out its assigned portions prior to the end of the month, it had no recourse but to be creative. This meant either negotiating with other families who had not used up their quotas or having to supplement their diet with other food stuffs like tuna which were sold in the open market (por la libre).

There were other items, such as household goods, that were sold only to married couples. Around Cuban circles, we used to hear anecdotes that sought to explain the rationale for the elevated divorce rate in Cuba as having to do with creative individuals "gaming" the system for the sole purpose of being able to buy items that they could not get through ordinary means. There was some truth buried in these supposed anecdotes; however, the compelling reason, in my view, for the elevated divorce rate in Cuba had to do with the level of emancipation for Cuban women. A secondary reason perhaps was that getting a divorce through the court system was far too easy. By paying a small fee, a marriage could be dissolved in less than a month. If there were children between the couple, for the most part the mother retained custody.

The constitution of the state guaranteed women equal rights in every aspect of life. I found Cuban women to be unique in insisting upon the equality of the sexes. Given that women integrated the labor force almost in a one-to-one ratio with men, they insisted on having men share the chores at home. One thing I noticed very early upon arrival in Cuba was that women smoked and drank just like men did. At the time I was growing up in Zambia, we rarely saw women who drank or smoked except for the ones with doubtful morals. It was somewhat a cultural shock for me therefore to see how women in Cuba engaged in the same behaviors as men. Women cheated on men just as easily, if not more; as a matter of observation, Cuban men who wished to maintain peace with their spouses, knew better than not to invite them to social events, unless there was a compelling reason not to. Anything short of that was rarely tolerated by women in general. It was a sharp contrast to the abuse I witnessed growing up in Zambia. I would also cite the lack of religious upbringing and influence as a key contributor to the high divorce rate I saw in Cuba.

Other items, such as luxury goods, were only sold on the basis of performance merits at work. For instance, to buy a car, one had to prove oneself exceptional at work, based on a comprehensive review that included one's political and moral standings, coupled with achievements in the context of contributions to the revolutionary principles.

As foreigners, we did not participate in this arrangement. We could, however, purchase items from the dollar stores. Unfortunately, not all foreign students received stipends from their respective governments, which made it particularly challenging to cope with social pressures. We were respected as foreign students mostly because we had access to foreign currency and could buy merchandise from the West that Cubans could only dream of. Once a year, we were given a pair of shoes, two shirts, two pairs of pants, and underwear, in addition to a winter coat. Most of us foreigners simply chose to give these items away to our Cuban colleagues, whom we thought needed them more than we did. In addition to the clothes, we received a monthly stipend in Cuban pesos and several packs of cigarettes. It is worth noting that, at the time, smoking in Cuba was a national concern of major proportions. The public was unaware of the health risks associated with smoking, which leads me to say a word about the health care system, based on my observations at the time.

Health care in Cuba was "free." Every individual residing in Cuba had access to free health care. As foreigners, we could go to any health care establishment for treatment without paying a dime. Medication could be purchased for almost nothing with a medical prescription, and no appointments were required, except for more specialized services. Services were provided on a first-come, first-served basis. In some instances, for more complex procedures, patients were asked to return on a specified day as determined by the doctor. Dental and eye care services were also provided free of charge. The first time I saw a dentist in Cuba, I was pleasantly surprised that I did not have to pay a single cent for three molars that needed to be filled, scheduled over three visits. The only inconvenience sometimes was having to wait in a queue, but the wait times were very reasonable. I surmised rather early that Cuba, despite the economic embargo imposed on it, had a few things to teach the rest of the world—including the US, for that matter. Not having homeless people sleeping under bridges or underpasses was also a case in point.

Political manifestations were a common occurrence. I believe the first one that I ever attended had to do with a dispute between the US and one of the Caribbean islands. We were asked to leave our classrooms and gather in the assembly hall. Once there, we waited for the dean to provide further instructions. One of the teachers who spoke fluent English served as translator as the dean read a statement condemning the act of aggression on the part of the US against a poor and indefensible country, simply for exercising the right to self-determination. One of the students followed up with additional comments condemning the barbaric act on the part of the US. In the end, shouts of "Viva!" echoed across the entire hall from all of us attendees. This, I gathered, was a well thought out campaign aimed at creating political consciousness among cadres mostly from Third World countries in favor of the socialist system.

We spent the weekends trying to assimilate as much information about Havana as possible. Mostly, we frequented the hotels and interacted with a lot of tourists who were mostly Canadians and Europeans. Rarely, one would run into Americans. We visited common sites such as Lenin Park, museums, and other cultural locales. What surprised me most was just how accessible and affordable these places were. In the realm of music and dance, Cuba was simply exceptional. Cuban music and dance such as salsa, cha-cha-cha, and the like, soon became our favorites. To say that love for the arts is ingrained in the Cuban people would be an understatement.

It was not long afterward that we had the chance to see, in person, the revolutionary leader (Fidel Castro), whom we had heard and read so much about in the history texts, seen on TV, and were now learning about through the Spanish language program and the media. Fidel Castro was a towering figure, not just in Cuba but in much of Latin America and other Third World countries, given his ability to poke his finger against a great power right in his backyard. The Spanish language curriculum was interspersed with an array of anecdotes around how Fidel Castro rose to power. The lessons covered the pre-revolutionary period when Batista was in power as a puppet of the US, the self-imposed exile of Fidel Castro and his colleagues (including their return to Cuba), the failed assault on the Moncada Barracks, the ensuing trial and the pronouncement of the famous phrase "Condenádme, no importa. La historia me absolverá." (Condemn me if you must. It does not matter. History will absolve me.)

We were also treated to the successive events that brought Castro into power, the alignment of Cuba with the Soviet Union, the Cuban missile crisis, and of course, the invasion at Playa Giron, which the Cubans hail as a key event in the path toward creation of their new society. This was the single event that garnered respect for them on the international stage by orchestrating a resounding defeat of a US-led invasion. Following the victory at Playa Giron, it was notable how the Cuban people have always been on guard against potential invasions from the US. Military drills were conducted every so often to ensure that every single block of the homeland left no stone unturned in terms of military readiness. Without exception, all Cubans had the obligation to participate in neighborhood vigilance groups known as CDRs (Comité de Defensa Revolucionaria). A student in my class once asked our Spanish teacher what would happen to us, as foreigners, in the event of an attack from the US. Her response did not delve into details other than that we did not need to worry about that possibility, as we would be well taken care of.

On the day we were supposed to see Fidel Castro in person, we were ferried in buses to the Revolutionary plaza very early in the morning. The plaza was already full by the time we arrived. We found a corner that we reckoned would give us a fair chance of seeing the *comandante-en-jefe* (commander-in-chief) as he gave his speech on the dais. While we waited, we encountered several English-speaking people from the US and quickly engaged them in a conversation about the economic embargo. These were Castro sympathizers, and therefore, there was no contention in the exchange that followed.

Suddenly, as if out of nowhere, Fidel Castro appeared to cheers from the welcoming party on the podium and the entire plaza. He looked much taller than I had imagined, and when he finally spoke, it was a powerful delivery and a poignant rebuke, mostly of the United States' misplaced policies. When we got back to school later that afternoon, we saw the Cuban leader on TV, answering questions from an American reporter. It was notable just how defiant he was in his delivery of answers to the reporter's questions. I could not help but think that Cuba, despite the obvious, was an outstanding example and model to the rest of the Third World. Cuba's advances in eradicating illiteracy, fostering health care, and other social programs stood as an outstanding example of what was achievable through focused leadership and organization. I could not help but think that my own country had a lot of catching up to do.

It was not long thereafter that Zambia's president at the time, Dr. Kenneth Kaunda, visited Cuba, and we were privileged to have an audience with him. Being the first Zambian students to ever study in Cuba, we felt it was incumbent upon us to formulate relevant policy questions during the planned question-and-answer session. Specifically, as students, we wanted to know if this alignment with Cuba represented a shift in policy from a capitalist economy toward openness to elements of socialism. As I recall, the president deferred the question to one of the cabinet members in his entourage, who was quick to state that we should focus more on the sciences than ideology.

With the passing of time (about six months into the program), it became apparent that we were making good progress in our communication abilities in Spanish. At this point, we had mastered the fundamentals; the rest was entirely on us, in terms of practice. I liked to read at the time, and there was no shortage of reading materials, especially on political themes. Reading Spanish literature became my favorite hobby; I ingested as much political material as I could find on the book stands. At church, someone gave me a copy of a book by Helen G. White entitled *The Great Controversy* in Spanish. As soon as I started to read it, I was hooked and did not want to put it down. I took it with me to class, and when there was a dull moment in between classes, I read a few chapters. If class was cancelled or the instructor did not show up, I read until I was interrupted. I was drawn to the Adventist faith and found the writings of Helen G. White very inspirational in relation to end-time prophecies.

Through my interactions with the SDA church, I reached the conclusion that while freedom of religion existed in socialist Cuba, that was not the entire picture. I heard first-hand the testimonies of many Adventists who were given a hard time in the exercise of their faith regarding observance of Sabbath Day rituals. Acquiring construction materials for the churches to perform much-needed repairs was not considered a priority by the central government. Religious individuals were watched closely because it was generally believed that they were not loyal to revolutionary principles. My own experience was that when I told people that I was a Christian, alarms went off. Some made fun of me, but I was not swayed. I tried to remain true to my faith as much as it depended on me.

One other observation of interest during my first year in Cuba was that of white-black relations. Cubans were quick to point out that institutional racism did not exist, and I have to say that I agreed wholeheartedly. There were no systemic policies marginalizing minorities based on skin color. Isolated experiences on the street, however, painted an undesirable picture. One of my Zambian friends, while with a white Cuban girl on a date, ran into a group of youngsters riding bicycles. They openly shouted at him in no uncertain terms that black and white did not mix. To make sure that he got the message, they turned around and repeated themselves several times in his face. He resisted saying something in response, as he was outnumbered. On another occasion, while riding on the bus to town, I witnessed an incident in which the driver, who was black, asked a white boy not to get on because the bus was full. The racist vitriol that the white boy uttered in frustration was unbelievable and probably not worth repeating. The driver was so devastated that he asked everyone on board to get off the bus. Understandably, these were isolated experiences and did not constitute policy statements by the revolutionary government. It was worth noting, however, that racism against black people in general was still very much a work in progress.

With time, as I familiarized myself with Cuban idiosyncrasies, I was exposed to the idea on the street that, in the hierarchy of races, the blonde was considered the most accomplished race, and the Negro, the most inferior. It was common, therefore, to hear a white individual refer to a black person who did something stupid as not having evolved sufficiently to act prudently. Later, when I challenged one of the instructors to explain the reference to the term *pelo malo* (bad hair) in contrast with *pelo bueno* (good hair), she was unashamedly quick to point out that kinked hair was considered inferior and that this view was not a matter of personal belief. This was a definition consistent with how reputable hair salons characterized hair. It was hard for me to swallow her response, but I chose not to pursue that line of discussion any further.

My final observation in relation to Cuban society relates to the issue of prostitution (confounded by the system of dollar shops), which, like racism, was not condoned as a policy of the state. The reality on the ground was, however, quite different. As a foreigner, I very quickly understood that there was a segment of Cuban women who were interested in having relationships with foreigners purely on the basis that foreigners (extranjeros) had access to the *diplotiendas*. I would not dare to recount how many people approached me in person, asking if I could buy them something from the dollar shops in exchange for Cuban pesos. Some women were quite blunt about the issue, to the extent of even offering sexual favors in return as long as there was a promise of no one ever knowing about it. I surprised a few people every now and then by simply giving them what they asked for and then commenting that I did not expect anything in return. Those who harbored a sense of gratitude toward me became lifelong friends. I had learned not to judge people on the hypocritical scale in relation to their ideological principles. It was my firm belief that in the hierarchy of human needs and priorities, ideology was probably at the bottom rung. As humans, we all crave the same things in life. It was just unfortunate that through no fault of their own, Cubans did not have access to some of the things we were exposed to simply because of the country they were born in.

While on the subject of dollar shops, allow me to indulge the reader in a little background regarding the practice of students selling merchandise to the local people. As previously mentioned, the dollar shops interspersed throughout the island represented one of a series of creative responses by the Cuban government for subverting the economic embargo imposed by successive American administrations. Through the sale of merchandise from the West to foreigners, the

Cuban government had found a viable additional method of acquiring foreign currency. Unfortunately, what they were not prepared for was the possibility that students and other foreigners would buy merchandise from the dollar shops and then sell it at inflated prices to the locals. Without a doubt, engaging in this practice was illegal, but the demand for foreign goods was so high that it was almost impossible to resist. I tried as much as I could to stay away from such practices, but the pressure from willing buyers was enormous. It was not unusual to run into high-ranking government officials or members of the Communist Party who would befriend one with the sole purpose of later asking for the favor of acquiring a *pitusa* or another similar item for them. Simply put, a pitusa was a pair of jeans. These would range in price from about 15 to 30 US dollars and would fetch about 100 to 150 Cuban pesos on the black market, which ironically was the salary of an average worker. Doctors, who were the most highly paid workers in Cuba, made about 300 pesos per month. Incredibly, the Cuban Central Bank valued the peso higher than the dollar.

Cuban vernacular phrases were used to hide a sale from law enforcement personnel. For instance, to ask about the price of an item, one would say, "Como se llama eso?" (What is that item called?) The returned response might be "40 cañas" (40 sugarcanes). In this context, sugarcane was the currency denomination. I recall buying a pair of jeans for a doctor I was introduced to. He came across as a nice individual caught in a system he might not have been entirely happy with. I really had no appetite to charge him anything; I simply gave them to him as a gift. I don't know how many favors he advanced as tokens of appreciation, not to mention that each time I needed to see a doctor; I would simply head to his home.

Some of the thrills of being in a language school centered on the friendships we forged with some of the students from other countries, with cultural interplay and ethnic diversity representing the entire globe. The cultural and intellectual exchanges were illuminating. In that environment, we were able to learn about the issues that other countries were confronting, such as the plight of the Palestinian people.

There were also students from the Caribbean who communicated in a language I could never understand. It sounded like they were speaking in tongues; the Patois language they spoke was almost impossible for us to decipher accurately. However, their reggae and calypso music were irresistible. Incidentally, when Bob Marley passed away, a meeting of solidarity with the Jamaican students was convened. The camaraderie and unity we experienced was simply overwhelming. We were all united under a common goal of opposing the West, which too often did not look out for the interests of our poor nations. As one of our friends appropriately pointed out, the Cubans were taking a long-term initiative by investing in cadres from all over the world to create consciousness of the existing international relations and issues. As poor a country as Cuba was, what they were doing was remarkable, and therefore, we could not stand in judgement of their intentions. Rather, they were to be commended for taking the initiative to balance support in favor of an alternative to the status quo.

Time flew by very quickly. The academic year came to an abrupt end much sooner than I had anticipated. I was not totally fluent in Spanish, but I could hold a conversation with almost anyone. Having excelled in all my classes, I was recommended for the dean's list by my Spanish teacher. Little did I know that there were perks associated with that recognition, specifically an all-expense-paid trip to one of the eastern province resorts for a week. It was the first time I had ever left Havana. We were treated to an array of activities, including trips to historical sites and museums, musical events, dining at the various restaurants around the city, and much more. The itinerary also included plenty of leisure time to explore on our own or merely relax around the swimming pool and chat with the local people. Cubans are very conversational by nature and would go out of their way to engage a foreigner in a conversation. The only complaint I had was having to deal with the scorching August heat; otherwise, I thought the trip was quite a ball.

We returned to Havana to recount our experiences to our friends and continued vacationing until September. We took several trips to visit a series of parks, theaters, museums, Old Havana, beaches, and other sites too numerous to mention. If the intent was to showcase the successes of the revolution, there was little doubt that we were on board.

On the days when no trips were arranged by the school, we were free to do whatever we thought was in our best interests. Having attained basic Spanish conversation skills, Cuban *mulata* women were quite an inviting contrast to the Zambian women we were used to, as they were not shy about taking the initiative to approach a guy. This was women's liberation on steroids.

Shortly before the summer recess concluded, the listing of university allocations was posted. I came to learn that I would be attending school in the province of Holguin, in a small mining town, with four other Zambian compatriots. I was not too thrilled about the idea of leaving Havana, but I really had no option. Most of my college mates were staying in Havana. On the appointed day, we packed our bags and were driven to the main bus terminal. We were given bus vouchers and left on our own to catch the bus to our destination.

The trip took about fifteen hours. We mostly slept through the night and only awoke when the bus stopped at the major stations along the way. During the day, I took time to admire the landscape as I had done previously. It looked very different compared to the Zambian landscape; there were no dense forests or wild animals on the island to worry about. Much of the landscape was flat, with sporadic hills and mountains breaking the monotony. In the distance, one could see the ocean waves breaking against the land mass. What a beautiful spectacle to behold, especially for one raised in a country without a coastline.

Fig 9: At the language school in the outskirts of Havana

Fig 10: One of the farms in the vicinity of the language school.
In the background is the typical Cuban landscape.

Figure 11: Summer vacation trip to Holguin following
graduation from Spanish language school

CHAPTER 8
First Year

Upon arrival, we proceeded to present ourselves to the dean of foreign students, as instructed. Following an informal orientation with the dean's office, we were assigned our dormitories and walked through the formalities, such as meal tickets, class schedules, and other details. We found other African students there, who welcomed us with open arms. Among them was a student from Ethiopia, who later became a close associate and confidant. This was to be my home for the following five years of my life. The pastor of the Adventist church I had attended in Havana had contacted the pastor of the local church in my new town, and to my surprise, when I showed up at church on the first Saturday, he had all the information he needed to know about me.

My new school was in a small mining town with little infrastructure. There was not much to do in terms of entertainment. A segment of the population that worked in the town was known as Palestinian, given that they only worked for a limited duration and were constantly on the move. There were also quite a few Soviets living in the city as expatriates, providing consultation services in the technologies for the extraction of nickel. There were probably three to five restaurants in the city, all accessible by public transportation, which unfortunately was not very reliable. There was also a small airport right in the middle of the city, with daily flights to major cities within Cuba. The one dreaded feature of the city was the red clay soil, which made it impossible to wear light-colored clothing; the wind from the ocean would blow the dust everywhere, and so most of the buildings were soiled red. One had to be cautious to wipe away dust before sitting down in a classroom or, for that matter, contacting any surface.

Having completed the routines associated with orientation and registration, we started our classes around mid-September. I remember sitting next to a girl from Guantanamo during our first lecture. I thought she was cute. It was not long afterward that I noticed a chestnut-haired girl sitting in front of us in the same row of the lecture hall. The professor had asked a question and signaled to her for the response. It was her poise and commanding voice that caught my attention; her physique was tiny, but she exuded so much confidence and intelligence. When I got to know her over time, I discovered that, underneath it all, she was just another woman with insecurities and vulnerabilities; susceptible to the wounds of love as I would later learn. I don't have a clear memory of how our friendship started, but somewhere along the way, Trini and I were drawn to each other and started sitting next to each other in all our classes. One thing I appreciated about her was her candor and honesty; she did not mince words. She spoke her heart with little regard for diplomacy. I quickly learned that she was opposed to interracial marriages, citing the common refrain that birds of a feather flocked together. She was also very active in the youth political organization known as the Unión de Jóvenes Comunistas (Union of Communist Youth), or UJC. This was the youth vigilante organization that reported all purported acts against the Revolution. From the get-go, I made it very clear to her that I was a religious individual. Surprisingly, she did not raise any objections to that; as a matter of fact, she gave me reason to believe she might have harbored sentiments of Christian faith in her closet. Her final comment about the issue was that religion was tolerated in Cuba, which was the Communist Party's official position on matters pertaining to religious beliefs.

Trini introduced me to a few of her friends and, for that reason, I developed a circle of friends I could practice my Spanish with. There was a movie theater in town that we used to frequent during our leisure time. Occasionally, we would go out as a group to have dinner at one of the local restaurants. For the most part, I footed the bill for everyone in the group, which the girls really liked. As noted earlier, there was not much to do in the city by way of entertainment; we kept ourselves busy over the weekends by celebrating each other's birthdays or just organizing *fiestas*. There was a dance hall on campus, which was available for reservations made ahead of time. It did not take much to hold a party in Cuba; all we needed was a bottle of rum and some music. Cubans were quite a festive people, and dancing flowed in their veins. I was a shy and reticent individual when I arrived in Cuba, but my behavior began to change as I adapted to the Cuban environment. There was no doubt that hanging out with Trini contributed to my character transformation. She did her best to encourage me to talk, and before long, I had become a chatterbox. Not that my character changed, but I had found a genuine reason to come out of my shell and become more conversational. Out of tender, loving care, she referred to me as her Pollito (translated literally, "little chicken"). I took no offense but embraced and welcomed her feedback on an array of issues.

Trini was truly a genuine individual whose friendship I appreciated on every level. As time went by, she began to insist that I find a girlfriend, and she was prepared to point me out to some of her acquaintances if I so chose. I was not too eager on her being the intermediary, but I embraced the general idea of finding someone special. I went out with several of her hand-picked selections, one of whom I grew to like but it was not meant to be. Before long, she had found a boyfriend herself, and therefore we could not spend as much time together as we had before. I also found a "greener pasture" in a nearby town. She would visit occasionally, but when her father found out that she was dating a foreigner, he was not in the least impressed.

Living conditions were not as desirable as I would have liked; as foreigners, we had our own dormitories, partitioned into cubicles. Each cubicle had two bunk beds with four individuals per cubicle. On one side of the dormitory, there were toilet facilities and bathrooms. We did our own cleaning of the living quarters and toilet facilities, taking turns via a cleaning roster. Our building was located on the west end, close to where everyone went to deposit their trash, and each time a group of girls would pass by our building en route to the trash center, windows would open and shouts of "Leona!" (lioness) would go out almost in unison. I did not quite appreciate the association, but it was another one of those Cuban idiosyncrasies. The girls did not appear to take this behavior as offensive. Too often, however, they would laugh or say something "fresh" in response, which would trigger an exchange of friendly vulgarities.

As I got used to being around Cubans, I became aware that Cuban women had a keen sense for fragrances and mostly went out of their way to appreciate a guy wearing nice cologne. Every morning, I went to class wearing cologne with a scent that was alien to them, I would be surrounded by a swarm of girls passing all sorts of nice comments, such as "With that cologne you are wearing, I would love to spend the night with you." It is likely that some of the comments may have been serious, but I determined not to pay too much attention to that sort of flattery, as Cuban women in general tended to be a little hypocritical. The opposite was also true in terms of a guy with natural body odors. Nothing turned off a Cuban girl as easily as a guy with bodily odor; not only would she break all manner of contact, but she would also make sure that every woman on campus got to know what a pariah you were. Therefore, we trained ourselves to be sensitive in that regard, sometimes even wearing women's perfume because that was uniquely what was available at the dollar shop. Somehow, unsophisticated Cubans could not distinguish between men's cologne and women's perfume; they appreciated all fragrances alike. My favorite (in the line of women's perfume) was Anais Anais. It would drive all women in my classroom crazy.

In terms of male culture on campus, one of the most cherished places to be was a corner dubbed El Jurado (translated, "the place of judgment"), which was strategically located between the female dormitories and the dining hall. This was a place where guys congregated to judge women on a scale of beauty. Each time a girl would pass, the judges would assign her a score on a scale of two to five. Catcalls were abundant for the highest scorers, and the girls were embarrassed to walk through the Jurado unaccompanied. There were, however, some who knew they were perfect fives and were not at all perturbed by guys echoing a few *piropos* (catcalls). As a matter of fact, some of them appreciated being desired publicly. The queen of all the girls at the institute was one named Teresa, a mulata girl from Havana two years ahead of us. Every time she passed by, there was silence and respect uniquely for her. One of my Zambian schoolmates, Mumba, in a display of humorous talk, would comment about Teresa, saying, "I wouldn't care less even if she had AIDS. I would just tell God after the act, 'Now you can take me. My mission on earth has been accomplished.'" This was the same guy who took pride in what he termed "the law of aggregates." Based on his silly philosophy, he wished, at the end of his life span, to be judged on the merits of the aggregate number of women he would sleep with. His estimate at the time was in the order of half a mile if the women were to stand in line back to back.

Other than Teresa, there was Melba, a girl from Guantanamo with a wasp-shaped body. Unlike Teresa, she drew cheers, laughter, catcalls, and plain admiration. Wearing a pair of jeans and high heels, which mortal man could resist her charm? Amazingly, she was quite friendly, and so was Teresa. It was Trini who taught me how to compliment women using piropos. In Cuban vernacular, piropos were ice breakers, a way to approach a woman without intimidation. I found out over time that piropos never failed. The trick was in knowing which one was appropriate for the moment. If a girl liked yours, she usually turned around and smiled. That was the sure sign that she wanted to hear more. One that I still recall today went like this: "Mamacita, si cocinas como caminas, me como hasta la raspa." (Girl, if your cooking is as good as your walk, I will eat even up to what is stuck to the pot.)

El Jurado was a popular locale, especially during the first few months of a fresh intake of students. Consciously or unconsciously, I found myself drawn to the Jurado a few times, participating in this fun endeavor. We did it out of sheer fun, not disrespect for the girls, but there were a few that protested, specifically the black girls, who unfortunately scored the least in the eyes of the judges.

I observed that Cubans had a great sense of humor and always found a way to make jokes about almost anything. There was a sweet wine they dubbed *bájate* bloomer (underwear takeoff). I found out later that the reason for this designation had to do with the ease with which women took off their underwear under the influence of this specific wine. We were also introduced to an array of Cuban phrases with special meaning. For instance, the phrase *pescador submarino* (underwater fisherman) was used in a subtle context to refer to one skilled in the art of oral sex.

Drinking beer was a common pastime in the absence of other entertainment in the town. It was not long before I began to observe some of my foreign campus mates getting themselves caught up in the habit, some to the point of becoming near alcoholics as their behavior transcended into uncontrollable impulses. I recall seeing one of our friends from South Africa drink himself into oblivion (total blackout), walking back to school swaying from one side of the road to the other. Upon arrival at the school, he then took the opportunity to curse out all his enemies, domestic and foreign alike, as we watched in disbelief. Given the apartheid situation in South Africa at the time, we all felt very sympathetic, knowing that technically he had no country to return to upon graduation. There was also the case of one of my Zambian friends, who drank so excessively at a party we held off campus one weekend that he fell asleep near a creek without anyone knowing his whereabouts. When he was eventually found, we all breathed a sigh of relief, knowing that he could have rolled over and killed himself in an instant. On another occasion, I recall seeing one of our Zambian boys get up at night to go pee and, instead of heading to the ablution block, he headed into the hallway, relieving himself right there and then returning to sleep. I concluded that these were manifestations of coping with psychological issues in a new environment with hardly any supervision.

There were other inconveniences to put up with, such as fellow students bringing their girlfriends in the dormitories and having sex under the cover and privacy of a mosquito net, while the rest of us were trying to sleep. As a Christian, it was not easy for me to hide my disdain for such behavior, but in all fairness, there was nowhere for the couples to enjoy intimacy. Almost everyone who had a girlfriend was doing it in the dormitories. Unashamedly, this was the norm.

I continued to attend the Adventist church quite frequently until I discovered a Baptist congregation in the town and switched. Soon enough, I had made new friends with quite a few Christian brothers and sisters of the same faith. I felt very comfortable at the Baptist church more than I had at the Adventist church. When they found out that I liked to sing, on several occasions, they gave me the chance to sing a solo. At one point, we took a trip to Baracoa in the Guantanamo province to visit another Baptist congregation. We had a blast as I was reminded of the Scripture Union camps I had previously attended in Zambia while in high school. Being at church in the company of other Christians made me feel protected, but being at school and exposed to the constant barrage of temptations was more than concerning. I kept wondering how long it would be before I would see my Christian values begin to erode and ultimately become compromised. I immersed myself into school and church as much as I could, but I had to agree that my life was lonely. Not having someone special was proving to be quite a challenge on the social sphere. I prayed for the strength to endure all manner of temptations that I was exposed to in my new environment. Vices like drinking were not an issue for me, but feminine beauty was a huge temptation I found hard to resist. In that environment, there were beautiful girls in every direction.

Coming from church one evening, I boarded the wrong bus but resolved to stay on until the last stop, where I would board another bus that would take me back to school. Seated in one of the back-row seats, I noticed a girl I had seen at church. When our eyes met, she smiled at me instantly, and I immediately walked back and introduced myself. When she said she already knew me from church, I was a little startled. We had a great conversation, which abruptly came to an end when she reached her destination. Before she got off her seat, which was next to mine, she made a poignant comment to the effect that maybe a beautiful girl would take over her seat. We both laughed heartily, and it was certain that we had made a connection. As I continued my trip to school, I started dreaming about the possibilities ahead. Olivia was beautiful in every sense of the word. She was raised in a Christian home and therefore embraced strong principles and values. It was quite refreshing meeting a girl like her in the Cuban environment. When she later introduced me to her mother, I finally understood where she drew her values from.

As we grew to know each other and time passed, I finally declared my true intentions to her, but she was not kind at all. She made it crystal clear that anything outside the confines of a true friendship would not go far. I agreed with her on principle, but deep down, I hoped for more. For now, at least, friendship was all I could hope for, as much as I liked her. We continued to see each other at church and whenever I chose to visit—under the watchful eye of her mother and the rest of the family. One day she surprised me with a signed copy of her birthday picture, which I had seen previously and asked for several times. She was as beautiful as an angel with her long dark hair and blue eyes.

Fiestas at school were a common pastime over the weekends. As foreign students, we had music systems that our fellow Cuban students could only dream of. For that reason, requests to lend our music systems for the parties were interminable. This translated into automatic attendance to many parties over the weekends. We were introduced to international Latin pop stars, such as Camilo Sesto, Roberto Carlos, and Lucia Mendez, not to mention local bands of the likes of Irakere and Los Van Van, whose music added that extra flavor to the fiestas.

The first year went by very quickly; we wrote our final exams around the June–July time frame. The dean of foreign students arranged for us to travel to Varadero beach for a week as part of our vacation. This was one of the most famous beaches on the island of Cuba, so the place was packed with tourists from all over the world and students from across the country. It was quite exciting to be among so many people, and of course, there was no shortage of women to talk to. We slept in tents erected right at the beach. We played beach volleyball, ran in the sand, and did anything else we could think of doing for fun. Of course, there were also those awkward moments when one would run into a couple making love on the beach in the cover of darkness or in tents in broad daylight. At the end of the week, it was sad to be finally leaving the "paradise" we had been treated to for an entire week. I had survived my first year in school without much fanfare.

Fig 12: Monument to Dr Antonio Jimenez in front of the University (ISMM) where I attended undergraduate school

Figure 13: Sharing a precious moment with several classmates in Cuba during my first year at the institute.

CHAPTER 9
Second Year

The one interesting development at the start of the second year was that we received a cohort of Zambian students at the institute. There was at the time a total of twelve Zambian students at my school. Given this development, it made sense to organize ourselves more effectively so we could not only better represent our immediate interests but also showcase our country to the other foreign students and the Cuban community at large. I had led the Zambian group the prior year. Some of our minor successes during the first year included representing our country in the celebration for the independence of Zimbabwe, the celebration of the anniversary of the OAU, and of course, our own country's independence. The celebrations mostly included speeches of solidarity, a demonstration of some of our cultural dances and recitations of poetry with political and cultural undertones. Now that the group was larger, we thought we could do even more to educate our peers on what Zambia was all about. I took the lead on behalf of our group to research political materials for the four to five speeches I was expected to give throughout the year. I became a speechwriter out of convenience, inspired by the likes of Fidel Castro and other Cuban political orators. When my friends from Zambia got the opportunity to listen to my speeches, they thought that perhaps I was harboring political ambitions upon returning to Zambia.

Among the new intake of Zambian students joining my school was a young man named Sichone, who shared my faith. Prior to leaving Zambia, one of the Christian brothers had given him my name and asked him to look me up upon arrival in Cuba, and this he did. I was elated to learn that he would be attending the same school as me; I immediately introduced him to the Christian brothers at school and inducted him into the community. We bonded right from the beginning and established a great friendship. Having him around was an answer to prayer. In him, I found a brother I could pray with and just talk to on any issue of concern. We did our best to encourage and support each other despite the exposure to much temptation all around us. He was a charming guy in many respects, and women found him irresistible. Not only was he popular with the girls in school, but folks at church also found themselves drawn to him, given his conversational skills. There was just an aura of charisma and charm about him that made people gravitate toward him.

Our senior Christian friend from Ethiopia introduced us to a Seventh-Day Adventist family living a few miles from school, within walking distance. The love and hospitality they showed us as a family throughout our schooling was unbelievable. Never had I seen such a spirit of selflessness from strangers; they treated us like family. We were free to go in and out of their home as we wished. Despite the system of food rationing prevalent in Cuban society at the time, they were quick to share their meagre portions with us when we complained of being hungry. At one point, I recall struggling with a chronic headache, probably aggravated by the immoral conditions I was exposed to. As late in the day as it was, I went to their home and asked to spend the night there till my headache had subsided. They quickly made room for me, prayed with me, and insisted that I not return to the school campus until I had completely recovered. These are the angels that God in His wisdom strategically places in our walk to accomplish His divine will and purpose. I never did anything of significance for them. They were just happy to be a blessing in the service of the Master. Their example inspired me to be considerate of other people's needs. Without a doubt, the example they set for us was worth emulating and made me a better person over time.

The first cultural event we celebrated during my second year was the twenty-first anniversary of the founding of the Organization for African Unity; deferred from May to September. The text of the speech in its original Spanish and the corresponding English translation can be found in the Appendix section. Consistent with the general themes of African unity, I also sought to highlight some of the issues standing in the way of our economic progress as the dark continent pertinent to the external debt, issues of apartheid in Southern Africa, and our desire to align the future of our fragile democracies with nations supportive of our self-determination.

The next opportunity presented itself in the celebration of the twentieth anniversary of Zambia's independence. Once more, the text of the speech in its original Spanish and the corresponding English translation can be found in the Appendix section. The referenced speech was presented with the goal of educating our colleagues about Zambia in general and did not necessarily represent a policy speech approved by the Zambian government. It was merely a summary of what I understood to be the essence of our history, economic achievements since independence, unfair trading practices with the west, and general foreign policies of solidarity and support for the total emancipation of the African continent. It was also an opportunity to thank the Cuban nation for the role it was playing in shaping cadres for the long term.

As part of the curriculum, we had to take mandatory communism classes for about six semesters. The classes were called the Philosophy of Marxism and Leninism. Without a doubt, these classes were an attempt at indoctrination in the belief that the spiritual realm or dimension is in essence man's creation and therefore every attempt should be made to re-orient the masses in the direction of dialectic materialism. According to this philosophical view of the world, scientific discovery should be based solely in the realm of the material world. In other words, whatever cannot be reduced to the level of molecules and atoms, such as belief in God, should be viewed with skepticism at minimum. I was not shy about letting my classmates and instructors alike know that I believed in God and did not see my belief as denial of scientific theory. Quite to the contrary, I argued with my instructors that my belief in God was personal and that it is not only what one can perceive that can be explained. It made for interesting discussions both inside and outside the classroom; I do recall one of the instructors making a mockery of the Virgin birth by asking me directly to explain if God the Father had slept with Mary to give birth to Christ. I thought the question as framed was blasphemy, rather offensive and ignorant, by reducing the Creator to having a sexual act with His own created being. My response was that I was not prepared to have that discussion with him; he was free to believe as he pleased. I thought he sensed my irritation as he quickly changed the topic of discussion.

Some of the topics in the philosophy of Marxism and Leninism proved quite interesting, such as the theory of truth, the fact that our understanding of the world is imperfect, and that as we learn more about the world, we discover that what is true today may not be so tomorrow. Therefore, knowledge should be framed in the relative context. There were also controversial topics, such as the evolution of society from capitalism through socialism, toward communism, wherein an individual would give to society based on his ability and would take from society based on his needs. One of my classmates, in a light-hearted moment (I presume) dared to ask the instructor if, under a communist society, men would be free to have as many women as they desired. The instructor did not, of course, answer the question directly. He only speculated that our needs would also evolve from the mundane to the sublime. The idea of a utopia on earth was so farfetched that it boiled down to a belief system similar to a religion.

In the study of Marxist-Leninist theory, perhaps my favorite topic was the role of the government in regulating human relations. The point of essence boiled down to what constituted intrusion by a government upon individual freedoms versus what was in the best interests of society. A parallel subtopic of interest in this context was the role of the government in striking the right balance in terms of safeguarding minority interests while still protecting the dictatorship of the majority (peasant classes). After all the discussions we had on these and other related topics, I came to the conclusion that an ideal government that responded to the needs of its people here on earth had not yet been conceived and probably never will be until God's kingdom comes.

Upon the completion of my second year, I traveled to various cities across the country, visiting Cuban classmates and other Zambian students interspersed all over the island. This was an opportunity to learn more about the Cuban people and their culture. Cubans in general were open to welcoming foreigners in their homes and sharing with them whatever little they had. Of course, it was during these visits that one would hear unhinged sentiments in relation to the so called *logros de la revolución* (achievements of the revolution). I travelled to Santiago de Cuba on the southeast coast of Cuba. This was the birthplace of the Cuban Revolution in 1959. From there, I travelled to Bayamo for a few days visiting with a small group of Zambians studying veterinary sciences. I then ventured to see the Bay of Cienfuegos on the southern coast; given its reputation for scenic beauty, I was not disappointed. Leaving Cienfuegos, I headed into Havana to spend time with some of the Zambians studying there. What I appreciated about traveling around the island was that it was relatively safe and inexpensive.

I had developed a keen friendship with a Zambia student by the name of McWale, who was studying at one of the local institutes. McWale and I had bonded, as he was a friendly individual with a wicked sense of humor. He had a magnetic personality with women, which he used to his advantage. Having lived in Havana for about three years by then, he was familiar with the major and minor streets in the city, including the locations where *putas* (prostitutes) used to operate. It was probably on the second day of my visit that McWale suggested an outing for a fun evening. I had no idea what he had in mind but went along anyway. Wearing our best cologne, we boarded the bus and headed toward central Havana. Arriving in downtown Havana, we walked toward the Havana Libre Hotel. A short distance into the walk, he asked me to walk ahead and secure a table at the restaurant while he took care of some business. He later appeared with two beautiful "chicks" who would be keeping us company for the rest of the evening. One of the girls was white with blond hair, while the other was a mulata; both were very beautiful. Being the *pioro* (white flesh lover) he was, the blond girl was his, and that was not up for negotiation.

Over the course of dinner, the girls asked us if we could buy them something from the dollar shop in the hotel. I was about to respond when he signaled to me to stay quiet as he would handle that specific line of conversation.

"That's not a problem at all. As soon as dinner is over, we will take care of that," he quickly responded.

"However, as you both know, the exchange has to be equitable, right?" The blond girl was quick to add, "Claro, me das lo tuyo y te daré lo mío." (Of course, you give me what is yours, and I will give you what is mine.)

Just like that, the deal was sealed. I looked at my friend as he smiled approvingly. We picked up the merchandise for the girls while they waited outside the shop. The mulata girl was about to grab the package from my friend's hands, but he resisted.

"Not so fast," he insisted smilingly.

At that point, the mulata girl asked where we would take them for the rest of the evening. McWale suggested a *posada* he was familiar with in the vicinity, but it turned out to be overcrowded that evening. A posada was essentially a low-cost motel, where couples could enjoy intimacy for the duration there were willing to pay for. One of the girls suggested that we could go to her parents' house, as they both worked during the night and she was the only child. We took a cab to her house, which was about forty-five minutes away. It was a night to remember.

The thrill about being at school in summertime during the holidays was that none of the Cuban students were around; mostly, it would be just us foreigners. One of the "cool" things that McWale would do just prior to the end of the semester was organize extra meal tickets for friends visiting from other parts of the island. For that reason, he always had visitors, not to mention that he was a great host and entertainer. We entertained ourselves playing soccer in the summer heat or going to the beach. One of the students we played soccer with was from another African country. He was quite a popular guy with Cuban women, but given his looks, I failed to connect the dots for his popularity until McWale put things in perspective for me. It turns out that the guy with a body stature like mine had a dick the size of a rhino's horn, and as crazy as Cuban women were, they all wanted a piece of it or him. Somehow, news travelled far, and women he had never heard of would show up at the gate, looking for him. Some simply wanted to satisfy their curiosity by seeing what they had heard, and in turn, they would offer to have him do whatever he wished to them.

There was not an African who did not want to be associated with him in the hope of gathering leftovers. It was the analogy of a lion that has eaten to its satisfaction but with meat left over for the hyenas. For one, he had put the reputation of the African homeland on the heights, and if that were the only contribution that Africa would be recognized for, it was not a bad start at all. Had he lived in the Western world he would have undoubtedly commanded a business empire earning top dollars simply for being well endowed. Maybe that was the partial answer to the million-dollar question framed in terms of what women really want; it confirmed the popular Cuban saying we used to hear on the street: "Se prefiere un caballo grande, ande o no ande." (A big horse is the preferred choice, whether it moves or does not.)

In the evenings, we would gather with colleagues from other countries around vino dulce (sweet wine), rum (such as Aguardiente, Caney Añejo, or Havana Club), and *pio pio* (fried chicken); tell good stories; and just enjoy plain old laughter. I was not a drinker by any stretch of the imagination; alcohol had never been my forte. I was just there to enjoy the camaraderie. Put together a group of young men and women with raging hormones to enjoy an evening, and a lot would happen prior to the break of dawn. On one evening I recall, as we gathered around some food and drinks, we suddenly started to hear what sounded like a woman sobbing from the room next door. Thinking that she was being abused by someone, we all rushed to the door in an attempt to intervene. Somehow, the sobbing was rhythmic and did not quite sound like abuse was involved. Realizing what was happening, we all looked at each other in embarrassment and cracked up in laughter as we turned around and walked away. One of the girls from South America in our company commented in laughter that she hoped she could find a guy who would make her cry to a similar degree. There was a challenge on the table, but none of us was brave enough to rise to the task.

Within the circle of friends we associated with was a girl from one of the Portuguese-speaking countries in Africa who had lived in Portugal. When I laid my eyes on her for the first time, I became as stupid as a dog; she was tall and slender, with a waist the size of a wasp. I asked McWale if I could date her. He encouraged me to try my luck, but when I did, she would beat about the bush and comment that she wasn't so sure how a long-distance relationship would work since I was not a student in Havana. I kept insisting until one day she admitted that she had a crush on McWale, even though she knew that he was dating another girl. Recognizing that sometimes that was the way the cookie crumbled, I moved on to other pastures.

One of the hot spots I had not yet explored in Havana was a popular nightclub called Tropicana, which was commonly touted a "paradise" under the stars. Being at Tropicana was thought to be comparable to a celestial experience, in the opinion of frequent attendees. I got my first opportunity to visit by way of an invitation from a colleague who had been there several times before. I had nothing going on that weekend and therefore obliged with enthusiasm; I was quite ecstatic to be visiting one of the hottest, most popular venues in the city of Havana.

We arrived at Tropicana after a short walk from the bus station and immediately noticed a bevy of unaccompanied women hanging around the area. They were in search of tourists to hang out with for the evening. During the pre-revolutionary era, this was one of the places that attracted a lot of American tourists. In the post-revolutionary era, the tourists were mostly Canadian and European. They were transported to the locale from the various hotels across the city in modern air-conditioned buses. We were ushered in and shown a table for four. My friend had extracurricular plans in mind that I was not aware of. He unceremoniously excused himself, showing up a short while later with two nice-looking Cuban girls. Before long, we were having drinks and getting to know each other. He focused his attention on one of them, and by inclination, I gravitated my conversational skills toward the other, summoning my limited Spanish knowledge skills to the best of my ability.

Out of curiosity, I asked the girl next to me if this was something she did frequently. Her response piqued my interest.

In a rather cavalier tone, she responded thus: "I am young, beautiful, and certainly have every right to enjoy myself like any other young person. Do you have a problem with that?"

"Of course not," I quickly retorted, trying to force a smile. "It may well be that you did not capture the essence of my question, and I apologize for my unintended offense. What I really meant to ask was whether you come to Tropicana frequently."

Sensing my embarrassment, she smiled back and assured me that she had perfectly understood the premise of my query. That turned out to be an ice breaker of sorts. We carried on the conversation rather fluidly following that awkward exchange. I went on to explain that I was attending school in another province of Cuba, and the conversation then turned to the politics of the revolution. I could tell she was uncomfortable with the idea of discussing politics, especially in that public forum. After a brief pause, I asked if she had any siblings, to which she responded in the affirmative.

"How about parents?" I asked.

She said "Yes" and quickly avoided making eye contact.

I then commented that I hoped I would have the pleasure of meeting them one day. Staring at me directly, she remarked that her parents lived in Miami and that she did not have much contact with them. At the time, I had only a vague idea that there was a colony of Cubans living in the US, but she was probably the first individual I had met since my arrival in Cuba with a direct story of being separated from close family. I proceeded to ask a series of follow-up questions to keep the conversation going. Her responses were getting rather emotional until she finally said what was on her mind.

"You asked me earlier if I come here often. To be frank with you, I do. I am here almost every weekend. The reason I come here every weekend lies in the hope of meeting a tourist who may be willing to marry me and take me out of Cuba. It is probably the only chance I have of being reunited with my parents."

"Family separations are never easy," I interjected, merely to convey the thought that I was listening.

By this time, I could tell that she was beginning to tear up as we sat in silence watching the show that was now in progress. I leaned in her direction, commenting that she should not worry too much, that God was going to grant her the wishes of her heart. This encounter had quite an effect on me. I understood maybe for the first time the reality of manipulated politics to the detriment of family unity. The poor girl had brought home the point that, amid all the revolutionary slogans, the chords of family unity continue to be the one common denominator we all seem to cherish as humans, irrespective of our identity or ideology. It could have been me in a similar predicament, separated from family with no hope of reunification except as determined by the whims of politicians. I had no easy answers, just food for thought. As we rode the bus back to school, I immersed myself in thought reflecting over the events of the evening. I was certainly thrilled with the "paradise" under the stars, but the "Tropicana" of my dreams was still a shimmering image.

I returned to my school after my vacation, contemplating all the thrills I had enjoyed in Havana. It was a memorable vacation in many respects, but it was now time to focus on the year ahead. It was safe to state that I had fallen in love with the island nation—perhaps not the ideology, but the people, their culture, and way of life. At the core of Cuban society were real human needs that I could identify with. What was different from my own society was, perhaps, the choice for the organization and administration of the same human needs.

Figure 14: Entrance to Tropicana Club, touted as a paradise under the stars (Courtesy of Tropicana Club Picture Gallery)

Figure 15: Showtime at Tropicana Club (Courtesy of Tropicana Club Picture Gallery)

CHAPTER 10
Third Year

One of the most significant developments during my third year at the institute was the construction of a new hotel, several hundred feet from where the school was situated. The excitement about a new hotel in town was quite palpable; indeed, this was going to be the first modern hotel in the city. As students, we were more than elated about the prospect of a new construction project right in our backyard. I do not recall how long it took to build the hotel, but it must have been around a year at most. At every opportunity, on our way to town, we would stop to review the progress, sometimes chatting with the construction workers to determine when building would be completed. It was probably toward the end of my third year when the hotel finally opened. The opening of the hotel was significant in many ways, but for us foreigners specifically, it facilitated new opportunities to sell merchandise acquired from the dollar shops to the local people.

While the Cuban peso could not buy you much, it could most certainly allow you to stay at a hotel for a determined duration. If, for instance, you sold two pairs of *pitusas*, you could stay in a hotel with that money for a week, accompanied by a beautiful mulata *criolla*, eating above average food compared to your peers in school. This was the lure at our disposal, and with hotel Miraflores in our backyard, I found myself slowly beginning to compromise my core values.

Following the end of the first semester, I traveled to the province of Camaguey to check on Kofi, with whom I used to attend church during our time in language school. This was prior to the internet age, and therefore, communication with him was at best sporadic. But during my visit, we found the time to catch up. In talking to him, it became clear that both of us had had experiences that were not so desirable from the Christian perspective. The lure of beautiful Cuban women was indeed quite a stumbling block. Rather than stay at school with him, he proposed staying at a local hotel as he had also wanted to contact some people in the US. I found out to my surprise that he had been approached by several church members with families in the US about the possibility of him going to visit their relatives there, with the ultimate goal of being their intermediary in terms of whatever items they wished to send to their families in Cuba. I marveled at the idea; visiting the US was nothing I had ever dreamed of since arriving in Cuba.

My friend was always several steps ahead, as he was already thinking about what was possible after graduation. On that same night that he was trying to call someone in the US, he began to relate the essence of his strategy.

"First, we need to establish contact with families in the US," he explained. "Once we get to know our US contacts, we will arrange a visit, with the promise to help transfer whatever items they may need to send to their families in Cuba. The best part is that once we are successful the first time, they will trust us, and we can establish networks. In the end, we will convey our intentions of wanting to migrate to the US upon graduation." He leaned back in the chair, smiling as he finished explaining himself. Then he asked, "What do you think?"

I quickly responded that I was totally on board with the idea.

Placing a call to the US at the time was only possible through a hotel establishment, and one had to go through an operator. The process took forever. On that day, we waited for close to four hours to get through. When the exchange operator finally called our room to let us know that the requested call had gone through, my friend jumped with excitement. True to his plan, he sweet-talked the gentleman on the other end of the line, making the case that we could be trusted to serve as intermediaries. The US contact sounded very receptive to the idea and could not wait for us to get there.

I don't believe that I slept well that night, as thoughts of visiting the US kept robbing me of my sleep. Before we retired to bed, out of nowhere, Kofi had arranged to have two beautiful women keep us company for the rest of the night.

I returned to my school with a lot to think about but kept the matter entirely to myself. We had agreed that Kofi would travel by himself at the end of the second semester, during the summer recess. I would be joining him the following year; the big hurdle was, of course, obtaining a US tourist visa.

The second semester went by too quickly for me; it was primarily because, based on the terms of our scholarship with the Zambian government, we were allowed one visit to Zambia and that year, it was our turn. I could not describe the excitement I felt when the semester finally ended. Perhaps the most significant motivation for me was being able to see my mother, whom I had not seen in almost four years. Given the unique differences in school closure schedules, our tickets were flexible enough to allow us to pick the dates of travel and the countries to pass through. I opted for flights through Madrid and London, having hooked up with several colleagues studying in Havana, McWale being one of them. We had arranged to stay in London for a few days to do some shopping, and certainly, London did not disappoint.

We arrived in Zambia and soon dispersed to our various destinations. I stayed in Lusaka for a few days with one of my cousins. At the time, my parents had retired and returned to their home village. My siblings were scattered in several parts of the Copperbelt Province. I sent word to my brother that I had arrived and was en route to the Copperbelt; he would be waiting for me at the bus station upon arrival. I reconnected with all three of my siblings and gave to each one of them the few gifts I had bought in London. After visiting a few other friends and relatives, it was time to return to Lusaka to for the trip to my parents' home. The sense of urgency on my part was quite palpable.

I had never been to my parents' home village and was a little apprehensive about the prospect of traveling alone. Fortunately, my cousin was able to find some people who were going in the same direction and arranged for me to travel with them. We got to the main town late at night, but I still had a few more miles to go to get to the village. Based on the instructions I was provided, I needed to inquire about the residence of an uncle of mine upon arrival, spend the night with him, and then ask one of his kids to take me to the village the following day. As planned, the following morning, we set off on foot. It took us about thirty minutes to get there. My father was home when we arrived, and when he saw and recognized me from a distance, he ran toward me and gave me a bear hug. We both had tears in our eyes and could not speak for a while; he was clearly elated to see me, and so was I to see him. He led me to the living room of the house he had built over the years while we were growing up. I asked for the chance to see the rest of the house, and he quickly obliged, showing me around. Later, we sat down and began to talk. He asked many questions, mostly about my welfare, but I was the one who was keen on knowing how they were doing in retirement. He did not have much to say, as I quickly sensed that they were struggling economically.

My mother was not home when I arrived. She had gone to a nearby village to visit her relatives. Following our short conversation, my dad excused himself, got on a bicycle, and raced to notify my mom of the news that her beloved son had arrived. While I waited, my thoughts raced back to the last time I had seen her at the hospital. I was not sure what to expect, but I was thankful that she was still alive; the good Lord had heard my prayer. As I stood up to wait, I knew that it was only a matter of time before I would have the chance to hug her again and never wish to let go.

Subconsciously, probably out of anxiety, I started to walk in the direction where I thought she would be coming from. Suddenly, she appeared in the distance running toward me, her shoes in her hands. She looked frail but still full of life. From where I stood, I could tell she had lost weight. In that moment, before I even had the opportunity to hug her, I burst into tears, crying uncontrollably out of mixed emotions buried so deep and for so long. It appeared that her first sense of duty was to calm my fears and provide assurance that she was alive and well. It was a hug for the ages, probably the last opportunity I would ever get to embrace her in that manner.

After a week of catching up, it was soon time to return to Lusaka for the long trip back to school. Before I left, I gave my mother the little pocket money I had left (about a hundred pounds) with the promise that I would do better the next time around. She could not hide her gratitude; she tightly held my hand and prayed for me, asking the good Lord for special favor upon my life. It was tough leaving her, as it was likely that this would be the last time I would ever see her. In the end, I cherished the joy of the blessing to be able to see both of my parents alive. The Good Shepherd had once again proved Himself true and faithful to his promises. As I rode the bus back to Lusaka, there was only one thought going through my mind. I needed to graduate in a hurry because more than ever, my parents desperately needed my support.

CHAPTER 11
Fourth Year

Upon my return to school for my fourth year, I found that the Hotel Miraflores was officially open for business. Little did I know that my life was about to change drastically as a result. Like other curious students, I took a self-guided tour to explore all the available amenities within the hotel. I was not disappointed; there was a swimming pool in the center with swim-up bar service, a spacious restaurant on the second floor, and a dollar shop. There were also administration offices on the second and third floors. The rooms were spacious, consisting mostly of two queen-size beds. The suites had, in addition, a sitting area. I was about to return to school when it occurred to me that I needed a few toiletries from the dollar store, so I stopped by the shop, picked up a few items, and proceeded to check out. The cashier was a beautiful Russian lady who, to my surprise, spoke fluent Spanish. She smiled often and was very polite. I asked what her name was, and she hesitated a little, smiling sheepishly.

"Do you smoke?" she asked.

"No," I responded. "Why do you ask?"

"I was just about to take a break and was wondering if you would join me briefly for a cigarette," she explained.

"Well, I don't smoke, but I'll pick up a pack of menthol cigarettes for you. While you smoke, maybe we can chat," I said.

Extending her arm for a handshake, she said, "My name is Mila. What's yours?"

"Abel," I responded.

We proceeded to exchange other pleasantries, and shortly thereafter, she locked the dollar shop to take a break. "Come with me," she suggested.

I followed her as she led me to the fourth floor, where there were a couple of administrative offices. She lit a cigarette and began to smoke, puffing the smoke away from me as I started to ask her questions about her country, family, how she found herself in Cuba, and so on. She turned out to be a good storyteller, a passionate and rather down-to-earth individual. She asked a few questions about my life in Cuba and Zambia, and I answered as candidly as I could. In the end, we had a great conversation, but like all good things, this one too had to come to an end. Without further ado, I asked if it was possible to see her again. She agreed without hesitation, noting that I knew where to find her.

As I walked back to school, I pondered the significance of this experience and where it would lead to. There were, however, two obstacles of concern that I could not resolve. First, although emotionally and physically detached from her husband, she was not legally divorced. She had met her husband, who was at the time a student in the former Soviet Union. They got married and subsequently moved to Cuba. My other concern was that she was a few years older than me.

The following day, I stopped by, and we continued the conversation. Within a week of meeting almost every day, it became clear that we had both reached a point of no return.

Mila was beautiful, tender, soft-spoken, and almost shy. To put it succinctly, she was fearfully and wonderfully made—that is, in the image of angels. She communicated at a very deep level; this was probably what attracted me to her the most. She came across as honest and true to her feelings. While she was mature, she was playful and fun-loving. I did not appreciate her smoking, but I was so drunk with love that I began to rationalize our relationship, overlooking the obvious. I was totally confused. Before long, we had consumed the forbidden fruit, and my confusion was elevated to an even higher level. Undoubtedly, the whispers and rumors did not take long to start circulating. I confided in one of my closest Zambian friends. I told him what was going on and waited for his reaction. To a certain extent, getting some things off my chest was liberating, but instead of keeping the secret, my confidant thought it was a story for the headlines. When my good friend Sichone found out, he left a note in my locker saying that he was praying for me. That was all he had to say on the subject.

My choice to ignore the obvious haunted me every day. One day, I asked Mila if we could talk. She had anticipated my concerns before we even started talking. She started off by recounting how she had met her husband and all the issues they had been through since their marriage. Having finished her story, she went on to say that she had made up her mind and was ready to marry me. While I appreciated her honesty, I did not think I was ready for marriage. For one, I had neither income nor a place to live. Her response was that she would cover all household expenses. In the days, weeks, and months following, she kept insisting on getting married, but my response was always the same. I cannot say she gave up, but she was patient, thinking that I would give in with time.

As we grew to know each other more, she asked if she could pay me a visit at school on a Saturday evening. I had my doubts but thought that I could accommodate her request. Fortunately, most of my dormitory mates usually went out on Saturdays. I therefore concluded that it was not going to be a great inconvenience. On the appointed day and hour, she showed up, carrying a picnic basket stuffed with all kinds of goodies from Russia. The few dormitory mates who were around went out of their way to accommodate my privacy, but secretly, they were jeering. Some even invoked the name of a popular US evangelist as a parallel. It was quite certain that I had lost the moral compass to show them a better way and ultimately the love of God because of my irresponsible behavior. Unfortunately, there was not much I could do to alter the shame I had brought on the name of Christ, the name I had professed to hold in high esteem. That was unfortunately the sway that women have had with men throughout the ages. My name was just added to the long list of victims.

As if this experience was not enough, I found myself in another compromising situation within the same time frame. In terms of background, one of our Zambian friends had a Cuban girlfriend who used to live (with her mother) not too far from the school I attended. As a couple, they were constantly fighting, breaking up, and getting back together. The cycles of breakups happened routinely, but each time they would break up, she would look for me and ask me to intervene, which I did to the best of my ability. It was surprising to see the girl show up at our dormitory one evening, asking for me. She indicated that she had something to tell me and asked if I could walk her home as it was already getting dark. I had homework to do that evening but agreed to hear what she had to say. As we walked, she recounted how she had broken up with her boyfriend again. I kept insisting that she should give him another chance, but she was adamant that she wanted to move on with her life. We were about half a mile from her house when out of nowhere, it started raining heavily. Fortunately, or unfortunately, there were a few edifices in construction close by, and we hurried to take shelter in one of the buildings while waiting for the rain to subside. We stood there chatting, and then suddenly without notice, she started to kiss me aggressively and passionately pulling off my shirt and pants. It was a move I did not see coming. I was somewhat embarrassed but made no attempt to stop her. She had moved too quickly, bringing me to the point of becoming a willing participant once the ice was broken. In the end, I gave her what she wanted, thinking that was the end of it, but it was not to be.

A month later, she was back to let me know that I was going to be a father. Not only was I shocked, but I was devastated; I did not know what to say initially. I suggested we table the matter for later discussion as I was too busy with schoolwork. The following day, I went to see her at her mother's house to discuss our options. I asked if she would consider terminating the pregnancy, given the unique set of circumstances leading to its conception and the fact that there was no relationship between us other than friendship and a child in the making. She indicated that she was not prepared to end the pregnancy, arguing that the baby would be the only reminder she would have of me. Seeing that the conversation was not going anywhere, I left with a weight on my mind. Following a couple of weeks of no communication, she showed up to tell me that she had thought things through and had moved forward with terminating the pregnancy. We both cried uncontrollably. It was a painful experience.

I told Mila about the incident. I thought her reaction was somewhat surprising. She was not in the least bothered, pointing out that I had been taken for a ride in relation to the pregnancy. She was adamant that the girl had only been bluffing regarding the pregnancy. Her only concluding suggestion was that I should not be so trusting of other women.

As time went by, Mila introduced me to some of her Russian friends, who were either married to Cubans or working as expatriates. Some of them were taking evening classes at the same school I attended, and therefore, we ran into each other quite often. As I grew to know them, I discovered what fun-loving people they were. On one occasion, one of them extended an invitation for dinner at her home. I asked if I could take Mila with me, but she thought it would be best if I showed up by myself. When I arrived for dinner, I expected to find her husband home but coincidentally, he had left town that same day in the morning. She cooked a delicious blend of vegetables garnished with herbs and spices, handing me a glass of wine before the meal. It was a lovely dinner; she exceeded my expectations as a conversationalist and host. I was just about to excuse myself to return to school when she indicated that she had a question for me.

She delved straight to the point, asking if I knew that she liked me. I understood in that moment why she did not want me to bring Mila along. She was a good friend, and I did not want to hurt her feelings, but I knew where she was going with that line of inquiry. I responded that I liked her, too, but only as a friend. She went on to explain that she had a fantasy about making love with a black guy and saw me as her chance of a lifetime. I laughed, putting her at ease as she thought of what to say next. The only thing going through my mind at that point was that I needed to find an exit strategy, an excuse allowing me to wiggle out of that situation without hurting her feelings. I let her know that I understood, but was totally unprepared, adding that perhaps there might be room for her request on another occasion. She seemed satisfied with that arrangement and agreed to let me go. I had escaped the lure of Jezebel.

Upon completion of the first semester in my 4th year, my goal and focus were to obtain a tourist visa to be able to travel to the US. While the US did not have an embassy in Cuba, they had a section of interests within the Swiss embassy. The place was heavily guarded, given the many attempts there had been previously regarding Cubans wishing to seek political asylum. The street on which the Swiss embassy was located was a common venue for political protests against the US government.

I decided to travel to Havana during the recess at the end of the semester. My friend Kofi, who had traveled to the US the previous year, provided meaningful advice regarding what to expect. I arrived at the US section of interests around 10:00 a.m. and was led inside by a US marine. After subjecting me to a series of search protocols, he inquired about the reason for my visit. I explained that I was there to apply for a Tourist visa to travel to Miami, and I went on to say that I was a fourth year, student and was exploring the possibility of attending graduate school in the US. He asked for my passport and then suggested that I wait for a brief period. Fortunately for me, there were only a few people that day. He returned with additional forms and asked that I fill them in completely. I turned in the completed forms and was told to wait for an interview that same day. When my turn came, I was ushered into the interview room to wait for the interviewer. As he walked in, I stood up and extended my arm for a handshake, and he shook my hand in return. As he sat down, he asked for my motivation for wanting to visit the US; I repeated blow by blow what I had explained to the marine.

"So what assurance can you provide to justify that you won't be staying in the US indefinitely?" he asked.

I explained that first I had no intentions of trashing the five years I had invested into my education in Cuba. Secondly, I was under obligation to return to Zambia based on contractual obligations with the Zambian government, to which he asked that I provide evidence of such documentation. I reached into my briefcase and produced the paper he had asked for.

To cut a long story short, he stamped my passport and handed it back to me, stating that he hoped I would enjoy my visit. I thanked him and tried very hard not to show any emotions, but inside I was about to jump through the roof. I walked out hurriedly, heading toward the nearest bus station.

For the entire duration of the second semester, I dreamed almost every day about what it would be like when I arrived in Miami. Except for my closest associates, I did not divulge my plans to any other soul. My friend in Camaguey was elated to learn that I had obtained my visa; the next step was to buy an airline ticket, but for that, I did not have to rush, as there were almost daily flights to Miami from Havana operated by Eastern Airlines.

I told Mila about my plans to visit the US and showed her the visa, but she was not thrilled, as she had heard many negatives about the US in general. I reminded her that I was simply going to visit and would be back in no time. It was hard to focus on studies with the anticipation of a visit to the US; however, I did my best to try to stay in the moment, keeping myself busy with schoolwork. Over the weekend, Mila was a breath of fresh air. I would see her at the dollar shop and when she needed to take a break, we would take the stairs leading to the administrator's office on the fourth floor. This was our hideout that no one knew about. We would sit there talk and simply enjoy each other's company. It wasn't long before the hotel administrator found out about what we thought was a perfect hideout. Sitting on the stairs one day, minding our own business, he suddenly appeared, heading toward the office. The only way he could get in was for us to make way for him by getting up. We politely rose to our feet and allowed him to pass through. It was quite an embarrassing moment, but our hideout could no longer provide the privacy we previously thought we had.

Despite my moral failings, I continued to attend church regularly. One day, I asked Mila if she had any misgivings about the Christian faith. She recounted that as a kid in Russia, she used to attend church, but religion was not really her thing. When I asked if she would be willing to attend church with me, she did not see a problem, but I did. Clearly, we both enjoyed each other's company.

She was very thoughtful, considerate, loving, caring, and communicative in addition to many other qualities that I truly desired in a woman but this was not an investment for the future, and I think we both understood that. She had asked numerous times about taking the next step toward marriage, but I had rebuffed her overtures every time with what she thought were lame excuses. She stopped talking about any plans and just went with the flow. There were some things that we both thought about but simply suppressed our true feelings for each other, as they were unresolvable for the most part.

No sooner had the second semester ended than I hurried to Havana to meet my friend Kofi. We made our final arrangements with folks in the church who had family in the US. They provided contact information in the form of phone numbers and addresses. One of the girls in my class had told me previously that she had a brother and other family in the US. They had left Cuba during the Mariel exodus of 1980. She had not seen her brother and the other family members for a very long time and asked if I would be kind enough to contact them, especially her brother. In a way, we were providing a useful service, connecting families. However, there were those who thought what we were doing amounted to contra-revolutionary acts, as I would later learn the hard way.

Having completed all the arrangements for the trip, we boarded a flight to Miami on a Saturday morning. The ninety-mile flight from Cuba took less than thirty-five minutes. As soon as the plane reached its highest ascent, it started to descend almost immediately. I had a window seat, and therefore kept looking outside to catch a glimpse of the city of Miami as soon as it was in plain view. In the distance, I could see the city as we began to descend. It was unfathomable that I had found myself in the USA; this was the country I had heard was a world power. To think that in only a few minutes, I would be touching down on US soil was surreal. I started to wonder at that point just what a blessing and privilege it was to have the opportunity of a lifetime. We landed without incident and started to disembark. As we got into the terminal, everything around me looked dazzling. The contrast between what I was accustomed to in Cuba and what I was exposed to then was comparable to night and day. However, there was no guarantee that we were going to clear immigration despite having obtained visas from the American Section of Interests. What I did not realize was that flights from Cuba were subjected to unusual screening and scrutiny, for obvious reasons.

As we entered the immigration checkpoints, Kofi and I were separated from each other and were subjected to intense questioning, involving everything from where we were going to stay to whether we were members of the Communist Party. I felt a little anxious answering all the unanticipated questions. To my relief, Kofi had just been cleared and saw me in the next room. He stopped and indicated to the immigration official that we were traveling together. Seeing him provided an injection of much-needed relief and confidence. Eventually, we were cleared. Unfortunately, there was another student traveling on the same flight that was not so lucky and was detained and sent back to Cuba on the following flight. My colleague looked at me straight in the eye and remarked with jubilance that we had arrived in the USA—La Yuma (as the Cubans commonly referred to it.) I was free to curse Fidel Castro or even Ronald Reagan for that matter if I chose to without fear of recrimination. I smiled back, acknowledging his assertion.

We picked up our luggage and proceeded to the exit gate where our contact would supposedly be waiting for us. As expected, someone shouted out Kofi's name as we stepped out, recognizing him from his previous trip. What a relief! He quickly led us to his car parked in the terminal parking lot. Soon, we were on our way to his house, a short distance from the airport, about twenty to twenty-five minutes' drive. As we drove, our host explained that he lived in an area called Hialeah, translated to mean "the city that progresses." We arrived at the house without incident. Since it was Saturday, family members were just arriving home from church. In the tradition of SDA members, lunch would have been prepared the previous day; all they needed to do was warm up the food. There were other young people they had invited to meet us at the house. The food, I thought, was good, but even more interesting was the fellowship we shared that day. I was already feeling at home.

Later that afternoon, we were driven to another home where we would be staying for the duration of our visit. The house was modest but had all the necessary amenities. Kofi and I were asked to share a bedroom. During the day, the man and his wife would go to work and leave us home. We would then cook our own meals, make phone calls to other contacts who would stop by the house to see us based on their convenience. Sometimes, they would take us out if time was at their disposal. One of the families we really grew to like was the family of the girl who was my classmate, Leonora. As soon as I called Leonora's brother and mentioned that I was a friend of his sister, he was filled with so much joy that he made effort without hesitation to meet us. We became friends instantly, as he took us to meet the rest of his extended family that same day. They were such nice people, and we really felt at home in their company. One of his cousins ran a courier service company; I believe he was the one individual to whom I attribute my decision to move to the USA following graduation. Out of curiosity, I had asked him what it took to open his business. He gave me a long answer that spanned his arrival from Cuba, and the struggles he went through to be able to put food on the table for his family. If one considers the fact that he did not have a college degree, it was clear that he had done very well for himself. He then proceeded to ask if we had any plans to migrate to the USA upon graduation. I responded that I, for one, had not given much thought to the idea.

Kofi indicated without hesitation that he had made up his mind a few years prior. At that point, he broke into a long discourse, citing examples of many of his acquaintances who had found their way to the US and were now in a better position to provide for their families back home. Skeptically, I asked about the process of acquiring a work visa. He suggested starting with a student visa to pursue graduate studies, and then finding a company willing to sponsor one. It was as if a light bulb went off in my head. The idea of getting into a graduate program was so appealing to me that I inquired for more information from him regarding schooling opportunities, scholarships and the like. While he did not have all the information, he suggested driving us to the University of Miami later that week if we were available. The friendship we had garnered with this one individual proved more valuable than I could have ever imagined.

During our three to four weeks stay in Miami, we got the chance to visit the most important sites in Miami, such as Bayside, Key Biscayne, Miami Beach, and Collins Avenue, among others. To ensure my trip was well documented, I took a lot of pictures using a Soviet-style camera I had purchased in Cuba. At the time, digital photography was not available. Most of the young people we associated with at church in Miami all seemed very happy with their decision to immigrate to the US. That, coupled with the fact that stories out of Zambia all painted a gloomy picture of the economy, not to mention the prevalence of HIV/AIDS, pushed me to consider the inevitable.

One of the places we did our shopping in Miami was at the flea market for the simple reason that the prices there were reasonable and sometimes negotiable. During one of those trips to the flea market, I made the acquaintance of Donna (a girl from the Bahamas), who had travelled to Miami to shop over the weekend. After a brief conversation, I learned that she frequently visited Miami, as the cost of items in the Bahamas was extortionate to a single mom of two. I asked for her contact information, which she provided without hesitation. Little did I know that she would be revealed as another angel lined up in my favor.

As with all good things, our time in Miami inevitably ran out. We packed a few suitcases, labeling what belonged to whom. Some other folks opted to send money to their families in exchange for a few dollars. It was time to return to Cuba. Our time in Miami had been well spent. Certainly, the possibility of making the US my next abode appeared to be within reach. We put on the new clothes we had bought, wore good cologne, and boarded the plane back to Cuba without incident. Our only concern then was being able to pass through the Cuban customs authorities without any suspicion that we were bringing in merchandise for Cubans. One of the customs officials was rather suspicious when he noticed the quantity of our luggage and asked his boss about it. His boss responded that if those were personal effects, we were allowed to bring in whatever we could. Not wishing to override his boss, he let us through without any additional questions. We had dodged a bullet, but it was not going to be the last obstacle.

For the items intended for the families in Havana, we did our best to distribute to the owners as quickly as time allowed. In the end, there were still some items that I needed to take to Guantanamo. However, as school was just about to start, I opted to take the items with me to school with the intent to find a free weekend when I could travel there.

One of the changes the Cuban government had implemented while I was in Miami was introducing another type of currency for the students, known as INTUR. This was done to mitigate rampant illegal practices. Based on the new regulation, students were required to convert whatever foreign exchange they had in their possession to the designated currency. When implementing this regulation, the authorities did not even consider a transition period.

Figure 16: Miraflores Hotel in Moa, situated a short distance from the university (courtesy of jeparsacuba.com)

Chapter 12
Fifth Year

Arriving at school, I was immediately surrounded by my Zambian friends, who wanted a detailed account about the US. I shared with them the pictures I had taken; I had also recorded some music on several FM stations, which I made available to them. Questions about the US were interminable. There were those who wanted to know if I had seen any of the big music stars, like Michael Jackson. On the other hand, there were those who wondered how I had survived racism in the US. I just had to ignore some of the questions that were being asked out of plain ignorance. As for clothes, I had bought quite a few, including what we dubbed at the time as Michael Jackson socks and a red jacket. I had become so popular that I was now a celebrity in my own right for the single reason that I had been to the US.

After the dust had settled, I traveled to Guantanamo to deliver the last of the items and the money. I stayed at the Guantanamo hotel while I located the recipients based on the addresses I had been provided. I had a few dollars in my briefcase and was not remotely concerned that I could be stopped and searched without a warrant. After all, this was still socialist Cuba. I was not sure who tipped the state security about my presence in Guantanamo. I do recall going into the dollar shop and purchasing a few items with dollars. I also recall having a friendly chat with two nurses earlier that day. One of them had asked if I could buy something for her in the dollar shop, which was nothing surprising. There was a knock on my door, and not suspecting anything unusual,

I stood up to go open the door. Two individuals in plain clothes identified themselves as being from the state security wing. They stormed into the room and asked me to identify all my belongings which they all carried with them to another room where I was asked to follow. They painstakingly removed every single item from my briefcase. At the end of the search, they wanted to know where the $500 in my briefcase came from. I responded that as a foreign student, I received a stipend from the Zambian government. Next, they wanted to know why I had not taken steps to convert the money into the allowed student currency. My answer certainly gave me away as I told them I had just returned from vacationing in the US. Now they wanted to know whom I had met with and whether the *contras* in Miami were using me to send things to their families in Cuba. The next thing I knew, I was being ushered downstairs to a waiting police car, which took me to a detention center. I was led into the main lobby of the detention center and later asked to follow one of the policemen. Before I could realize what had happened, I found myself alone in a cell. I had just been arrested; I tried to launch a complaint, but to no avail.

Three days later, I was told that my case was going to be resolved in the town where I attended school. All my money was confiscated. I don't even remember how I got to school. When I arrived at school, my Zambian schoolmates had heard that I had been arrested. There were some who cheered quietly because my arrest was a classic example of "pride before a fall." Equally, there was a multitude of sympathizers, who came to encourage me to stay strong.

There were rumors of me being expelled at any time. With only one year to go, expulsion seemed like a harsh punishment that did not fit the crime. I was a little concerned, but I had at least one friend in high places that I had done favors for previously. He was the Communist Party representative at the school level. Through his wife, I asked for an audience with him, but he was not too keen to meet with me in public; he asked to have all my questions channeled through his wife. Basically, he asked me to be transparent and repentant when I was called in to discuss my case.

On the appointed day, I was summoned before a panel of security officers at their main building, which was not too far from my school. To the best of my ability, I answered all their questions candidly and went on to plead for leniency and, at minimum, to be given the chance to graduate. I mentioned my ailing mother at home and cautioned that they would be sending her to an early grave if I was not allowed to continue my studies. I then delved into mitigating conduct in my favor, such as maintaining a high GPA, being the leader of the Zambian Association at my school, and generally being in good academic standing for the previous four years. Following my comments, I was asked to leave the room briefly while my fate was deliberated. In the end, I would have to forfeit the money I was found with but could continue my studies. I thanked them, reiterating that they had made the right decision.

I was already behind in my studies because of all the distraction; I spent the following few weeks playing catch-up. This was my fifth and final year. I tried to put behind me all the distractions. I was more determined than ever to move to the US following graduation. I told myself to stay focused on the goal. As time moved on, my life was back to normal. Throughout this trying period, Mila stood by my side and provided valuable support. Maybe she was another guardian angel sent to protect me.

Since there was now a strike on my record, I needed to be extremely careful regarding whom I associated with or sold merchandise to. Using intermediaries become my mode of operation; more like a "mafia" king. The money was indiscriminately used at the hotel for booking hotel rooms and buying food. It was rare that I ate from the school dining facilities. The most compelling motivation for engaging in selling merchandise was to avoid the conditions in the dormitories and supplement the repetitive diet at school. This was pretty much how I survived the entire fifth year. Unfortunately, our Cuban colleagues could only dream of this sort of lifestyle. Jokingly, they called us capitalists, but there was a connotation of truth to this assertion. We were sharks destroying their way of life.

Completion of the first semester of the fifth year was indicative of no more classes. The second semester was used exclusively for the thesis project, which one had to defend in front of a panel to be able to graduate. Depending on the project one was assigned, one had to balance time between traveling to the plant, doing experiments in the lab, and documenting the experimental findings in a presentable manner. For this project, I teamed up with a classmate from Zimbabwe to develop a theoretical model capable of predicting the extraction of nickel from ammonium carbonate liquor. Essentially, we had to develop a computer algorithm capable of performing material balances based on certain assumptions. In one sense, we were fortunate, because much of the work was going to be done in the school laboratory. One of our professors provided overall guidance; we met with him at least once a week to report on progress and discuss any issues. The assignment was challenging but very interesting. We worked hard at it, often going beyond the call of duty to be able to meet pressing deadlines.

Around the March time frame, I asked for permission to take off a week at minimum to travel to Havana with the intention of getting a visa to the US. Only my closest confidants knew the purpose of the trip. Having gone through the process once before, I was more than prepared this time around. Upon arrival at the American Section of Interests, I went through the same motions as the previous time, explaining that my motivation for a visa request was related to exploring opportunities for graduate studies in the US. I was able to produce all the requested support documentation. Once again, I got the visa, which was valid for six months. My plans were slowly beginning to fall into place; at this point, I knew there was no turning back.

My friend and I continued to work on developing a simulated algorithm for performing material balances. After several attempts, we produced a model that seemed to work appreciably well. We divided our tasks equally in the interest of time; while one worked on programming, the other would focus on literature searches and writing the introductory portions of the thesis. At the end of every week, our professor would review the work and provide meaningful advice.

Toward the end of the six-month period allotted for the thesis, we were finished, with about two weeks to spare. We then went ahead and scheduled our defense date, providing copies of the thesis to all members of the panel. I could sense that my tenure in Cuba was quickly coming to an end. My colleague and I started to plan our graduation party; we decided to book two adjacent suites at the hotel. The plan was to have lunch with key individuals who had supported us through our time in school. We tried to put together whatever funds we had to make the celebration a memorable occasion.

A few days prior to defending the thesis, I asked Mila if we could meet and talk. This was a conversation that she did not want to have. Without even telling her what I had in mind, she had sensed what was coming. She suggested I wait for her after work and then we could take a long walk and chat.

I did not have to tell her the obvious; she already knew I was about to graduate and would be leaving Cuba. I focused on letting her know that I would cherish her friendship for the rest of my life. I also attempted to let her know that if destiny worked in our favor, we would probably meet again. I tried to draw her attention to specific events that happened between the two of us and encouraged her to remember those events in moments of darkness and doubt. She talked very little, opting to listen for the most part.

At the end of the walk, she indicated that she would stop by school the following day. I waited for her with anticipation. When she finally arrived, I let her in. She had brought a bag, but I could not tell what was in it. She reached in and pulled out an album of the city of Saint Petersburg, handing it over to me. She then went on to explain that she wanted me to be reminded of the city she grew up in. It was a wonderful gesture. Next, she pulled out another piece of paper on which she had written a poem.

The poem read as follows:

"Que la tierra gire alrededor del sol; comoquiera nos encontraremos dentro de un o unos cuantos años. Que tu vida corra como un río; entre las orillas que florecen y que siempre vivan contigo esperanza, fe y amor; el agua pasa entre dos árboles pero sus raíces crecen juntos; el destino separa a dos amigos pero sus corazones viven juntos; mientras dure mi vida, no te olvidaré; en la vida puede suceder de todo; pero que no me olvides tampoco; ahora tú estás lejos, lejos; no te pongas triste ni tampoco me eches de menos; acuérdate de mí, mira el álbum y espero el día de nuestro encuentro."

"May the earth continue revolving around the sun; we will still meet in one or a few years. Let your life run like a river; between the banks that flourish and that hope, faith and love always live with you; water passes between two trees but their roots grow together; fate separates two friends but their hearts live together; While my life lasts I will not forget you; everything can happen in life; but don't forget me neither; now you are far, far away; don't be sad or miss me; remember me, look at the album and I look forward to the day we will meet again."

I kissed her on the cheek and told her how much I appreciated this gesture. She did not want to stay long, to give me time to review my thesis defense. I thanked her and saw her off.

The following day, we stood before a panel in the last academic exercise of my studies in Cuba. We were given about forty-five minutes to an hour to present our work, which was divided equally between the two of us. We allowed about fifteen minutes for questions and answers and then waited for the decision of the panel.

The panel awarded us the maximum points possible for originality, ingenuity, and scientific content of the thesis work. Following pronouncement of the final grade, my mate and I looked at each other and hugged spontaneously, both of us fighting tears. Just like that, it was over, and now it was time to go celebrate.

We all walked to the nearby Miraflores Hotel and were ushered into the restaurant by a smiling waitress. She led us to the tables previously reserved. Mila joined us a little later, but I was glad she did show up. My project mate and I both gave speeches of gratitude to our guests. I noted in particular the unwavering support of the lady who used to work as the administrator in our department. The woman had been a pillar of support for me since our initial meeting at the start of my first year. I was deeply indebted to her and her family. We then dismissed our guests and headed to our suites to wait for the evening party.

In the meantime, we bought a bottle of Spanish rum known as Fundador. The size of the bottle was peculiar in that it was larger than all the other rums sold in Cuba. We retired to one of the suites and started to drink. I was not known to be a drinker, but on this occasion, there was so much I needed to forget—my failures, arrest records, an abortion, and the many undesirable situations I was forced to deal with living in socialist Cuba. This was the only time in my life that I have ever got drunk. Truth be told, I was senselessly drunk by the time we finished the bottle around 6:00 p.m. Our guests began to arrive around 7:00 p.m. One of our Zambian friends volunteered to deliver his music system and play the role of designated DJ. My project mate had a girlfriend, who showed up with her sister and several other family members.

Mila did not show up until much later, and this was the embarrassing part I did not recall. I was told later that I tried to undress her in front of everyone but she slapped me hard several times, bringing me back under control. She opted not to stay, as she had other business to attend to. The madness continued for much of the night. I do not know how many other things I might have done or attempted to do as the party progressed. The following morning, I woke up sleeping next to a beautiful Cuban girl. Such was the madness of the night. The good news was that she was someone I had personally invited to the party.

Two to three weeks later, I took a trip to Havana to make final arrangements and then returned to school one more time to pick up all my belongings and bid farewell to all the wonderful people I would be leaving behind. The truth was that I had fallen in love with Cuba. Leaving was not going to be easy, but I needed to do it. I finally left, opting not to see Mila on the day I was due to leave. It was a painful decision not to see her for the last time, but I thought this was the best option for both of us. The feeling was surreal; the melancholy was overwhelming.

I proceeded to Havana and stayed with McWale while I arranged for my flight to Miami. It was in August of 1988 when I finally left. As I passed through immigration, one of the officials turned over to me and asked where I was going.

I responded, "Miami."

He retorted, "After educating you, now you turn against us to join our enemies?"

I could only smile back at him.

The second leg of my life had abruptly come to an end; I was leaving just as I had arrived—with nothing except for the knowledge in my head and the ability to speak Spanish. This time, the apprehension I harbored about the future was real. I had too many question marks in my mind and no easy answers. With only $450 in my pocket, I was going to need help desperately. A voice in my head kept telling me that this was what faith was all about—stepping out of the comfort zone, having the ability to see that God was going to come through in His own way and in His own time. As I boarded the plane, all I could think was "God, is this your plan for my life? Don't I have an obligation to go back to serve my people in Zambia? If you tell me no, I will get off the plane right now."

Of course, I did not get off the plane. Therefore, in a way, I had surrendered myself to His lead, mindful that it was both a fearful thing and a delight to subject oneself to His will. In that moment, the words of Isaiah the prophet echoed through my mind: "Have you not known? Have you not heard? The Everlasting God, the Lord, the Creator of the ends of the earth neither faints nor is weary. His understanding is unsearchable." As the plane gathered speed down the runway ready for takeoff, I rested in the thought that nothing was insurmountable for Him. As hopeful as I was for the future, I was sad to be leaving the island, the beautiful landscapes, its beautiful people, the friendships I had forged over a period of six years, the beautiful beaches, and of course, the beautiful women. I was reminded of a similar feeling of apprehension and anticipation when I had left Zambia six years prior, but in all fairness, this time, I was by myself, and that was quite a challenge to contemplate except in the context that "the just shall live by faith."

PART 3

Second Continent

CHAPTER 13
Life in a New Environment

The short flight to Miami was about to come to an end when the captain announced that we had begun to descend. I started to ponder what I was up against. Firstly, I was traveling alone, and if, for some reason, I should be detained or denied entry upon arrival, what the likely implications would be, I could not even begin to fathom. While my friend Kofi had left about two weeks prior and was already in Miami, I had not been able to contact him to confirm where I would be staying. Secondly, I only had a phone number of the individual I was supposed to contact upon arrival in Miami. If, for whatever reason, he did not pick up my call, I couldn't even begin to imagine the panic I would have to deal with. The only consolation against this backdrop was that I still had my flight ticket to Zambia.

We landed without any glitches. I took my time disembarking, as I was in no hurry to face immigration officials; it was almost 11:00 p.m. when we arrived. We were led toward the immigration line by no-nonsense-tolerating immigration staff, who maintained a close watch, perhaps because this was a flight from Cuba and the animosity between the two countries was well established. Fortunately, this time around, the lines were short. When my turn came up, I handed over my passport to the immigration officer, who asked where I would be staying. I responded that a friend from church was going to pick me up and that he lived in Hialeah. He further asked if I had been to Miami before, and I responded, "Yes, I was here last year." To confirm this assertion, he double-checked my passport and later handed it back to me. Just like that, I was on my way to Customs, where I was asked if I had anything to declare. Noticing that the Customs official was Cuban, I saw my first opportunity for a minor dose of humor, stating, "There is nothing of value to declare out of Cuba." He smiled and let me through. I was a free man. At minimum, my first prayer had been answered.

As we stepped out to a rowdy crowd of Cubans waiting to welcome their relatives, I walked straight to a public phone and dialed the number I had been given. Someone by the name of Moises answered the phone. I recognized his voice from the prior year's visit and proceeded to let him know that I had just arrived from Cuba and was at the airport, waiting to be picked up.

"Very well, Abel. I will be there in about twenty minutes," he assured me.

True to his word, he got there in about twenty-five minutes, apologizing for the slight delay due to the traffic. He waved at me as he pulled up at the curb in his Oldsmobile vehicle. After a brief exchange, he helped me with my luggage, and in no time, we were on the 836 Highway, heading toward the Palmetto Expressway. As we drove, he explained that he was taking me to the Delgado family, who were members of the church living in Carol City, to the northeast of the airport. Previously, my friend Kofi had alerted the relevant church members regarding my pending arrival. One of the ladies in the church had agreed to host me initially since her father lived in the same town where I had attended school in Cuba. It was past midnight when we finally arrived. The lady of the house responded to the knock on the door and ushered us in. Moises left almost immediately as he had to report to work the following day.

We sat in the living room, chatting for a little while. Mostly, she wanted to know how her father was doing. I assured her that he was in good health and that he was very appreciative of the items she had sent to him the prior year. She then proceeded to show me the bedroom I would be occupying and asked if I needed anything to eat. I thanked her for her hospitality but indicated that I was more tired than hungry. Before going back to sleep, she showed me the essential areas in the house, pointing out that she and her husband would be waking up early to go to work and that I would not see them till late in the evening.

With that, she excused herself and retired to bed. Before going to sleep, I knelt in prayer as was my custom and thanked Jehovah for his blessings and the human angels he had placed in my way to guide and protect me at every turn, as undeserving as I was. Just like that, the transition of my life's journey from the island to the North American continent had begun. It was late August of 1988. As they say in one of our Zambian languages, "Ifintu fisanga abaume" (For men, certain events are unavoidable.) The perceived meaning underlying this common Bemba phrase relates to absolute persistence in the face of adversity; that unique capacity for resilience to face whatever life throws at one without turning back. It was time to prove what I was really made of.

I woke up the following morning not knowing what I was going to do. My first order of business was to establish contact with Kofi, who had left Cuba ahead of me. After taking a shower and finding something to eat, I got on the phone and started calling the contacts we had established the prior year. Most of them were working, and therefore, it would be the weekend before they would be able to stop by. On one of the calls I had made that day, one of the brothers from church mentioned that he had seen my friend Kofi the previous week and could make a few calls to be able to provide the phone number of the folks he was staying with. It was a relief establishing contact with him; we made plans to meet that same day. As soon as the folks he was staying with showed up from work, he would ask them to drop him off. In the meantime, I stepped out of the house to survey my new neighborhood. It turned out not to be the best of neighborhoods; primarily, it was a black and Hispanic area with little by way of infrastructure, social amenities, or industries. Not too far from the house, within walking distance, was a strip mall with a few shops. Other than that, I did not notice anything of significance. Talking to someone at the strip mall, I found out that there was a bus service leading to the Miami downtown area.

The family hosting me had a son attending middle school. He returned home around 3:00 p.m. Finally, I had someone to talk to. He was a fine lad, rather curious, and asked a lot of questions about Cuba. We got along well right off the bat. When the parents showed up in the evening, we ate dinner together and had the chance to get to know each other a little more. They were nice people with hardly any academic credentials; the husband worked in a metal fabrication plant, while the wife worked in an assembly plant. I quickly took the opportunity to ask the husband if there were any job opportunities at his place of work. He thought that whatever was available was probably not in my area of interest.

While we chatted, there was a knock on the door. It turned out to be my friend Kofi. We were both very happy to be reunited. His presence just lit up the mood around the room. We talked animatedly, cracking jokes about Cuba but also reminiscing about the good experiences on the island.

In an unexpected move, Kofi turned to the hosts and asked them if it would be all right by them if he could stay there with me so we could keep each other company as we thought about what to do next. That was the character of my friend; he was bold, decisive, communicative, and just plain outgoing. He just had a way of winning friends and influencing people. Without any hesitation, the hosts agreed to the request. They were a family of modest means. In a way, I felt a little awkward, but considering that this arrangement was meant to be temporary, I reckoned that it would not be too much of a drag on their meager resources. By the next day, Kofi had completed the move-in arrangements. Sharing a bedroom allowed us to discuss our every move as we transitioned into the American life.

Over the weekend, some of the friends we had met the previous year showed up, mostly to greet us and provide encouragement for our pursuit of the American dream. We made it clear to everyone we ran into that we needed help to get to the next step. While they all thought that they knew someone who could help us find temporary jobs, the biggest obstacle was the difficulty in attaining work permits. This was the issue that was to haunt us for quite a while; we kept asking colleagues at church to help us find temporary jobs so we could make some money. It was then that I became aware that Cubans migrating to the US had special status and were granted automatic stay in the US upon arrival. They were unlike any other community of immigrants. That was probably sufficient explanation for their inability to suggest meaningful immigration alternatives. They did not have to worry about navigating the maze of US immigration law. As I saw it, our options were rather limited. Applying for political asylum was probably a non-starter as we had never experienced political oppression with our respective governments.

The other alternative that we thought we could consider pursuing was trying to obtain a student visa, but that required being able to demonstrate financial support. Finally, marrying a US citizen was probably the most certain of the available options. Kofi and I would spend sleepless nights analyzing and re-analyzing these and other options meticulously. At one point, Kofi suggested that he was going to apply for political asylum, as he came up with what he thought was a legitimate basis, and asked for my opinion. I found so many loopholes in the contemplated plan that I adamantly argued that he was ruining his future by attempting to go that route. What ensued subsequently was a protracted argument; we ended up not talking to each other for a couple of days.

My Zambian friend Sichone had just finished his fourth year of studies and had also traveled to the US before I left. I had anticipated seeing him at the SDA church in Hialeah at least once prior to his return to Cuba. He showed up the following weekend, but little did I know what he had been through. I found out that upon arrival, he was detained and sent to the Krome Detention Facility. The issue was brought to the attention of the pastor of the church, who quickly intervened on his behalf. He was released after just a few days, but that experience had shaken him a bit. My soul was surely glad to see him. We mingled as inseparable friends for much of the time, exploring the city and visiting other Cuban families for the duration of his stay. One of the folks he established contact with was a gentleman by the name of Miguel. Miguel had a son in Cuba and was keen on sending something to him through Sichone. Meeting him for the first time, it became obvious to me that Miguel knew the streets in Miami. As I talked to him more and more, it dawned on me that he might just be the person likely to suggest something meaningful, or at least point us in the right direction, but I sensed the need to wait for the right opportunity.

Sichone left for Cuba a few weeks later. I bought a couple of souvenir items and asked him to deliver them to Mila. Following his departure, I tried to keep myself busy during the week, taking the bus to downtown, where there was a public library. I tried to research several schools in the area in terms of requirements for admission into Graduate School Programs. At the library, I also took the opportunity to review employment listings in the local newspaper. It became clear to me that Miami was not big on industrial jobs; it catered more to the service industry. I reasoned that my best path forward would be to get into graduate school first and then look for a real job. However, I needed money to sustain myself as a priority. Since I did not have a work permit, my only option was to find a temporary job outside my scope of study with someone willing to pay me under the table.

Time kept ticking, and I found myself going through the same motions week after week. The weekends provided some relief in terms of opportunities to meet people at church, and target individuals who had small businesses for potential assistance. At some point, one of the contacts in my network whom we had met the prior year disclosed that he had a small vehicle that he wanted to get rid of and was willing to sell it for a few hundred dollars. My friend Kofi jumped on the opportunity by borrowing money from someone at church. Shortly afterward, we had the means of getting around the city. While the car was essentially his, I, too, benefited as we were together most of the time. Unfortunately, I could not drive, but at this point, I was desperate to learn.

One Saturday afternoon following the church service, we were introduced to two ladies who were friends. One was Cuban and the other Colombian. We started mingling as friends. The Cuban lady had her own apartment, and whenever opportunity presented itself, she would invite us to her home after church service, where we would have Sabbath dinner. Sometimes, we would go out as a group to various parts of the city. She had been in Miami for quite some time, and therefore, she was able to take us to different places. Her friend from Colombia had not been in the country that long and was still living with her parents. My friend Kofi perceived this friendship to be an answer to prayer at least for himself. He had made up his mind about tying the knot with the Cuban lady. When he discussed the issue with me one evening, I was caught off guard, but I understood his perspective. As his friend, I was a little concerned that he was making the decision of a lifetime in such a hurry.

Truth be told, Kofi had always been a pragmatic guy. Based on what I knew about him, I did not think it was in his nature to place too much weight on love emanating from feelings—emotional love as it were. From his perspective, he was motivated by the desire to find a solution to a prevailing problem, and that was all that mattered. Regardless of how much I disagreed with him, I understood what was at play. Several days after this discussion, he proposed to the woman, and without a second thought, she gave him an enthusiastic yes. He later discussed the issue with the church pastor, who was not the least bit surprised The pastor even offered to officiate at their wedding in due course.

Kofi wasted no time; it was a Saturday when he proposed, and the following Monday, they were at the courthouse, getting a marriage certificate. To make it official, they invited the pastor to the house, where they held a modest ceremony. I was happy for him, but the implications for me were profound. It meant that I would be alone with no access to transportation. Essentially, I would be stuck, not to mention the pressure I felt living in someone's house and contributing nothing. My friend Kofi hurriedly moved out to join his bride and started the process of applying for a work permit.

Not too long afterward, the lady of the house I was living in approached me and courteously indicated that her father would be coming from Cuba for a visit. She went on to say that it was her preference to have him occupy the bedroom I was using upon his arrival. She then asked what sort of plans I had for the future. It was a question I was not prepared for, but I understood where she was coming from. I asked her to give me a few days to think things through and get back to her. She assured me that her father was not coming immediately, but I knew she had done enough already. I was truly grateful for all they had done for me as a family. After all, it was not my intent to continue living in their house for an extended period. It was a long night when I went to sleep; I kept thinking about what made sense to do next. I thought about approaching the girl from Colombia and going down the same path my colleague Kofi had embarked on, but I could not reconcile that idea with my principles. Besides, she was not a citizen, and therefore, the legalization process would have taken forever. She was a good friend, but I didn't want to take advantage of her in that manner.

In my confusion, I remembered Miguel. With Sichone serving as an intermediary, we had met him a couple of times, and he had invited us to his home previously. Miguel lived in a good neighborhood in the southwest part of the city with his wife and two kids. I decided to call him and explain my dilemma. To my surprise, he told me not to worry; he would pick me up, and I could stay with him while I attempted to hatch my next move.

The following day, I thanked the Delgado family for their generosity and all they had done for me as I explained that I would be moving to stay with Miguel and his family. In a way, my problem was not resolved. I was simply transferring one level of guilt for another. Miguel and his family were kind to me. They had a two-bedroom townhouse and offered me the opportunity to sleep on a single bed in the same room with the kids, who shared a bunk bed. Their economic situation was not the best either, as Miguel did not have a steady job at the time. His wife worked at a day care center while he drove a truck, making fish deliveries across town. It was not long before I started feeling guilty again; to make matters worse, the bus service in the area was not the best. Too often I was stuck at home with nothing to do. When he drove to his routes selling fish to his clientele across the city, I went with him, but merely keeping him company was not doing anything for me. I was back to square one again and something needed to give.

When I was stuck at home with nothing to do, I would watch TV, fascinated by afternoon talk shows such as Geraldo, Sally Jesse Raphael, Jerry Springer, and of course, Oprah Winfrey (my favorite). What caught my attention the most was the ease and openness with which topics considered taboo in the society I was brought up in were discussed. This was indeed the land of the free that I had heard so much about. There seemed to be no boundaries around hot issues such as sex, marriage, homosexuality, and politics. It was a cultural shock for me to listen to a man or woman invite his/her significant other on a show, only to let them know in front of an entire national audience that there was somebody else in their relationship. I could not remotely grasp why anyone would see the need to put another through this sort of ordeal; I was dumbfounded at the excesses disguised as freedom of expression, the nasty dances I would watch on television, not to mention the disgust I would experience watching two guys kissing. It was all just too much for me to digest. I recall several years later inviting a girl I had just met on a one-day cruise docked in international waters. As we lay on the deck, watching the stars, she asked me if I had any fantasies that she should know about. Not knowing where she was going with this line of inquiry, I responded that I did not have any. She then confessed that she had one and asked if I wanted to hear it. Expectedly, I wanted to hear what it was. To my surprise, her fantasy was to have sex with two guys, one going in from the front and the other from the back. To cut a long story short, we never saw each other again following that cruise.

On another occasion, a girl I had a friendship with asked me if I knew what "golden love" was, to which I responded in the negative. She went on to explain that it was another level of closeness between lovers. It consisted of a couple making love either in a shower or bathtub and then defecating in each other's presence. I could not believe what I was hearing. Given my conservative background and ideas, this was another individual I could not think of associating with. Undoubtedly, I was not open-minded in my view of the world. I was brought up believing in right and wrong. Any experience that was not in my sphere of comfort, I frowned upon as wrong or evil. In short, I was intolerant and judgmental, but over time, through my interactions with people from other backgrounds and self-directed, open-minded reading, I started to embrace the idea that things were not always black and white. A shade of gray was certainly a reasonable option in some instances. I began to open up to the idea that, before walking in someone else's shoes, I should not be too quick to judge, as the word of God rightly teaches us.

Watching political discussions between Democrats and Republicans was something I really grew to appreciate. I found the ability to discuss diametrically opposed political viewpoints in a cordial fashion to be quite fascinating. Coincidentally, when I arrived in 1988, Mike Dukakis was running against George Bush in the presidential elections. For a while it seemed like Dukakis had the edge. How Bush was able to turn things around in his favor was a stroke of political genius. I watched the debates with keen interest, absorbing the main issues of the day. Being conservative in my viewpoints, I tended to side with the Republicans on the general issues of fiscal conservatism and limited government as espoused by the great statesman Ronald Reagan. I was fascinated by the ideas enshrined in the US constitution regarding inalienable human rights.

Every Sunday morning, I would listen to the political talk shows to hear the issues of the day debated candidly through the lenses of the two major political parties. The one idea that I failed to reconcile in my mind was seeing the evangelical movement (which I was a part of) align itself with the Republican Party. I was brought up believing the church should be apolitical. I could not grasp the essence of this alliance. I would listen to radio programs like "Focus on the Family" and was perturbed by what I perceived as the notion of Christians attempting to capture political power as the means to reforming society. Cognizant of my understanding of the teaching of the Word of God in terms of the weapons of welfare at our disposal, I came to the conclusion that this was not an argument I could support with a clear conscience as a Christian.

The principle of separation of church and state, in my opinion, was and continues to be consistent with the teaching of the Word of God. Allowing a religious group to take hold of political power opens a Pandora's box likely to disadvantage other religious groups. Another notion I could not reconcile with my own beliefs, or the symbol of Christ, was the staunch support I observed among evangelicals pertinent to the Second Amendment. While this was disguised as Christian values, it was American nationalism at best or pure hypocrisy at worst. Without saying much on the subject, I wondered why as Christians, we need extra protection in addition to what God has already promised. Over time, I distanced myself from the ideals of the Republican Party and began to align myself more with liberal causes, championing opportunities for the masses rather than the elite few. This view, I found to be more consistent with Christ's teaching in the sermon on the mount and in Matthew 25 of the Bible.

In the world of sports, I grew to appreciate watching NBA stars, such as Michael Jordan, Isaiah Thomas, and Magic Johnson, and the rivalry between their respective teams. Their level of play was a thing of beauty to watch; I used to wonder whether these individuals had inborn traits that the rest of us lacked. Hearing their stories in interviews, it was amazing to note just how much hard work elevated them to stardom. Somewhere in there was a lesson for me that the American promise could only be realized through sweat and tears.

Watching professional baseball was another passion I embraced. I was introduced to the game of baseball while in Cuba through watching the likes of Orestes Kindelan, Antonio Pacheco, and Victor Mesa (to name a few) playing at the amateur level. However, watching Major League baseball in the US was a dream come true for me, given my love and appreciation for the game.

There was no denying that I was falling in love with the US, and harbored deep-seated hope that one day I could be a part of the American experience. I could not see how things would eventually play out, but the good news was that America was the land of dreamers, and I had no shortage of dreams waiting to be fulfilled. I just needed to hold on to my dreams and pursue them with all my might and strength.

My visa was about to expire, but I had resolved nothing during my six-month stay. My first instinct was that I needed to buy more time. Donna, the girl I had met from the Bahamas during my first visit to the US, suddenly crossed my mind. Upon arrival in Miami, I had taken the initiative to let her know that I had arrived. On one or two occasions while staying with the Delgado family, she had traveled to Miami, and we had arranged to meet. "What if I traveled to the Bahamas, got another visa there, and then returned to the US?" I thought to myself. The idea seemed to make sense. I discussed it with her over the phone. She was eager to see me, and therefore, we agreed that I would travel to the Bahamas the following weekend and she would wait for me at the airport.

I bought a one-way ticket to the Bahamas and asked Kofi to pick me up and drive me to the airport. We did not talk much as we drove. I had told Miguel that I was going to try my chances in the Bahamas. He did not think it was a wise decision, but understanding my situation, he went along with it. Basically, I bid them farewell and left. Arriving at the airport, my friend accompanied me to the counter, where I attempted to check in. They asked for my passport and gave it back to me immediately, stating that I could not travel as my visa did not allow me to re-enter the US. It was probably divine intervention telling me that I was about to throw away my future. I tried to argue, but to no avail. I did not know what to do. How was I to go back to Miguel's house when I had already said goodbye? Kofi and I drove back in silence.

Miguel's wife was home, doing household chores. I explained that I was not allowed to travel, and understandably, she looked confused. She let me in, suggesting that I talk to Miguel upon his return. Kofi left immediately as he had other matters to attend to. Dropping off my luggage, I took a walk around the neighborhood prior to Miguel's return home. It was undoubtedly a low point in my life; I felt like giving up and returning to Zambia. On that same day, I received a letter from one Zambian friend I had studied with in Cuba, telling me just how bad things were back home. In his letter, he expressed how much he envied my courage for taking the bold step to try my luck in the US. He was curious about how things were working out for me. He also asked if I could send him a few dollars, as he had met the woman of his dreams and was hoping to get married later that year. I did not know how to react to the letter, but it was a reminder that I needed to count my blessings, all things considered. The thought of being an illegal immigrant, however, was profoundly preoccupying.

When one stops to consider the realm of potential cascading calamities that could ensue, one minor and unintended infraction of the law could lead to additional inquiries by authorities and, subsequently, jail time or deportation. I had to remind myself on several occasions that this was not the time to entertain negativity. The quintessential ingredients I was overlooking in my apparent logical analysis were faith and patience. I needed to dispel all manner of self-doubt from my psyche and recognize that the journey before me was not just about me, let alone my reputation. There were other stakeholders that I may not even have been aware of when one considers that the Master's blessings potentially impact generation upon generation. In that pensive mood, I was moved to write a poem in Spanish, which I titled "Los Comienzos Humildes" (meaning, "humble beginnings").

Con sedienta ansiedad, espero
Entre sueños y vislumbres de esperanza
Entre murmuras y suspiros
Espero el rayar del alba
Espero el amanecer
De un día luminoso
Un día que se esconde detrás de las nubes densas
Un día que ha de dar al traste
A las lágrimas e ilusiones
¿Sera mañana?
¿La próxima semana, mes, año? Tal vez
Solo sé que ha de llegar
Tarde o temprano
Mas se mofan de mí
Los que ojos de fe carecen
Pero en mi silencio, sé que el tiempo lo dirá todo
Cada día que nace
Me infunden nuevos alientos
Y esperanzas encendidas
Porque lluvia que no escampa, desconozco
Tarde o temprano
En las perlinas puertas, he de encontrarme.

With profound anxiety, I wait
Between dreams and glimpses of hope
Between murmurs and sighs
I wait for the break of dawn
I wait for the sunrise
Of a brighter day
A day that hides behind the dark clouds
A day that will bring an end
To the tears and illusions
Will it be tomorrow?
Next week, month, year? Probably
All I know is that it will be here
Sooner or later.
How they make a mockery of me
Those who lack eyes of faith
But in my silence, I know that time will tell it all
Every day that is born
Infuses me with renewed desire
And burning hope
Because of incessant rain, I know not
Sooner or later
At the golden gates, I shall arrive.

When Miguel returned home later that evening, he told me it was no problem to continue to stay with them. He urged me to be patient, but I felt bad having to find myself in this awkward position.

CHAPTER 14
Rays of Hope

Over the weekends, I would go with Miguel and his family to their church, where I would attempt to meet potential influencers likely to help. No one really appeared to suggest anything meaningful; as time continued ticking, I grew more and more desperate again. I recall waking up one Saturday morning and taking a walk around the neighborhood. I did not know where I was going; I just kept walking. I saw a park in front of me and walked in that direction. Seeing a bench in front of me, I sat down and just started to pour my heart out, asking God to open doors if this was His will and purpose for my life. I thought about my retired parents back home with their needs, and here I was, not able to help in any way. I was moved to tears. I made a solemn plea to the Almighty from the depth of my soul that I was not going to leave the park until I felt the blessed assurance that He had heard my cry, like Jacob, who contended with the man of God, saying, "I will not let go of you until you bless me." After what seemed like an eternity, I walked back to the house slowly and in peace with the assurance in my heart that God had heard my humble prayer.

That same evening, as Miguel was preparing dinner, one of his Colombian friends walked in to see him prepare ceviche, a Peruvian dish. I was introduced to him, and in that moment, Miguel asked his friend if he could think of a job for me at the construction site. The Colombian man responded that he could use a painter. I told him I had never painted before but would be happy to learn, and with that, he asked me to show up at the construction site the following

Monday. It was within walking distance, probably a couple of miles away. After almost six months of doing nothing, I was about to get a small break. Was this pure coincidence or answered prayer? This was another experience that affirmed my faith and belief that God was in control.

I showed up at the construction site early in the morning, where the patron met me to show me around. It was a residential construction project consisting of 120 units. Through a friend of his, the patron had been awarded the contract to provide painting services for all the houses in the community. There were two other Colombians, a Cuban, and another guy from Honduras working with him. My job was going to be painting the exterior while the other workers focused on the inside. In that sweltering Miami summer heat, I thought to myself how some things just never change; the black guy would always be relegated to the inferior role. But this was no time for complaints. He gave me a quick demo of how to paint and in no time at all, he asked me to take over as he watched me. He suggested a few pointers and then left me unattended. He later showed up to review my work, which he thought was satisfactory. He added that he would be paying me $140 per week. I did not complain. I just went with the flow. The thought of waking up to go and do honest work, as demeaning as it might have been for a college graduate, was for me a blessing. The work was tiring initially, but I soon got used to it. I thought that if I could maintain this pace, I would save enough money to find my own apartment down the line.

Out of every paycheck, I gave Miguel $50 as contribution for my upkeep. Certainly, what he was doing for me was much more than I was contributing. Following the first few paychecks, I put aside $100, which I sent to my parents. It was a proud moment for me to be able to send money to my parents for the first time. I also took the opportunity to write to them, assuring them that I was in good health, that they should not worry too much about me, and that I was adjusting to my new environment and hoping to get into graduate school with time.

My other priority was getting a driver's license. Fortunately, my coworkers at the construction site would occasionally allow me to practice driving in their vehicles—a favor for which I was very appreciative. When I felt comfortable driving, I contacted a driving school, and they agreed to pick me up to practice for a thirty-dollar fee per hour. Following several practice sessions, I decided it was time to take the road test, even though I was not completely proficient. I had previously taken the written test and only needed to clear the practical. My driving instructor, despite his initial protest that I was not ready, went with me as I would be using his car for the test. After an excruciating twenty minutes of driving with the traffic cop sitting next to me, I was told in the end that I had passed. With the driver's license in my hands, I was profoundly emotional while the instructor drove me home.

From then on, Miguel would let me drive his car, asking me to run errands for him; his son would often go with me for the ride. I was not where I wanted to be yet, but these seemingly minute blessings were beginning to add up. Every time I passed near that park where I had prayed and cried for special favor, I was reminded of God's goodness and faithfulness, as undeserving as I was. I remembered Jacob, who in his distress had held on to the man of God with all his might without letting go until he got the assurance that his blessing would be forthcoming.

In the summer of 1989, my friend and brother Sichone, wishing to follow in my footsteps, notified me that he had graduated and had obtained a visa to come to the US from Cuba. He asked if I could pick him up from the airport and make arrangements for him to stay in Miami for a few days prior to heading to California. I discussed the matter with Miguel, who seemed eager to see Sichone again as they had established a good rapport the previous year. On the appointed day, Miguel and I drove to the airport and picked him up as planned. It was refreshing to have my brother in Christ around. I left for work the following day while he stayed chatting with Miguel. Upon return from work, we found time to catch up on the relevant events related to Cuba and the mutual acquaintances we had left behind. It was a refreshing experience.

Before he left for California, I provided a few pointers regarding what to expect and look out for. He, too, was going to start his life in the US, living with a Cuban family. I suggested to him that he should focus on finding a job and moving out as soon as possible, mitigating some of the mistakes I had made when we arrived. He was fortunate in that the folks who had agreed to host him were small business owners, and therefore, his first job was already guaranteed. By the second week of his stay in Cali, he was already working and was able to move into his own apartment over a period of about three months. We stayed in touch and checked up on each other at least once every week.

Another angel that the Lord put in my way was a friend by the name of Juana. She was Cuban and very active in leftist politics. I recall being introduced to her by a mutual acquaintance whom I had run into when I first visited the US. We became friends instantly; she was probably the closest female friend I had at the time. Having been divorced from her husband, she was a single mom raising a daughter who was attending high school. When we both had the time, she would pick me up and we would go partying in different clubs around the city. We talked about politics, mostly about Cuba, and US policies of interference in Latin America. We did not always agree, but she had a compelling way of presenting her arguments, such that I always saw where she was coming from and ended up in her camp most of the time, regardless of the topic under discussion. For that reason, I used to affectionately call her "La Reina" (The Queen). She was a writer and was working on her first book when we first met. The depth and breadth of her knowledge made it pleasant to be around her; not only had she travelled extensively around the world, but she also knew the city of Miami very well. Each time we would go out, she would always suggest a new place to explore.

It was through her that I came to know the many hideouts dispersed throughout the city. Sometimes, she would ask other people to join us, mostly Brazilians she knew from her prior experience dating one of them. Through Juana, I came to know a girl from Bolivia who was at the time staying with her sister, married to a Brazilian. Elena and I grew to like each other. Surprisingly, she was a member of the Adventist church. I could not help but wonder why Adventists kept showing up in my life. We would talk over the phone late into the night. There was only one problem between us; both of us were immigrants with expired visas, and therefore, a meaningful relationship was essentially a pipe dream. Deep down, I knew she liked me, and I liked her too. I thought she harbored the hope that one day I would openly declare my love for her.

Unfortunately, that day never came. Her sister's husband had started to complain about her prolonged stay with them until she could no longer take it. One evening, she called to let me know that she was uncomfortable staying with her sister's family for so long and asked if I would consider living with her. Before I could answer, she went on to say that I was her last hope and if I could not, then she would pack up her bags and return to her country. Using all the empathy that I could muster, I explained that this proposition was a nonstarter, not feasible under our conditions at the time. By the following week, she had packed her bags and was on her way to the airport, where miraculously she met a Bolivian man at the airport who was so taken by her beauty that, when he discovered that she was returning home, he begged her to stay. She gave him a chance, and they got married almost immediately. When her sister called to tell me what had transpired, I was dumbfounded. I called her and wished her the very best in her journey. That was the last time we ever spoke.

One night, Juana picked me up to go to dinner somewhere around Key Biscayne. As we got into the car around 2:00 a.m. to return home, the car would not start. I was probably about thirty miles from where I used to live and wondered what options we had. It suddenly occurred to me to call my friend Kofi for a ride home. Reluctantly he agreed to pick us up. It was quite an inconvenience for him understandably. To my surprise, he showed up with his newly wedded wife, who did not look very happy. They drove us home, dropping off Juana first. Upon arrival, he asked to be reimbursed for gas money. I gave him a few dollars and thanked him for coming to our rescue. As much as we were good friends, I perceived that our relationship was not quite the same as before. I wasn't aware of what had changed. I just felt a little isolated from him but was determined to succeed on the Lord's timetable as He opened more doors for me. At this point, little did I know what the Lord had in store for me.

Several weeks later, my Bahamian girlfriend was in town for the weekend. That same weekend, another friend from Ghana who had been with us in Cuba invited me to his wedding in Miami Beach. He was marrying into a Cuban family from New York, and as a wedding gift, his future mother-in-law had rented a fancy house for them by the beach. My girlfriend had rented a car, which we used to drive to the wedding party. Around 8:00 p.m, we were driving to the wedding when we narrowly escaped what would have been a fatal crash. I was driving and realized abruptly that I was about to miss a turn when I decided in a split second to swerve into another lane, not realizing that another car was coming from behind on the same lane, moving at top speed. Noticing that my vehicle was already in front of his, the driver pressed the brakes as hard as he could to avoid the accident. My girlfriend, sitting next to me and seeing the car behind us, screamed at the top of her voice for me to accelerate in the hope of avoiding a hit from behind. At this point, we could hear the squeaking breaks as the car behind us came within inches of our car. I was visibly shaken and understood for the first time what it means to have your life flash in front of you.

As I pondered this experience, I understood just how precarious life could be. One moment you are on top of the world, and in the blink of an eye, it is all gone. I do not think I even enjoyed the wedding party that night. Seeing that I was in a pensive mood, my girlfriend decided to drive on our way back. As she drove, I found time to gather my thoughts. My friends were all getting married, and with that, opportunities were opening for them in terms of better-paying jobs. With those jobs, came the ability to buy housing, travel, and start families. It felt like I was the only one left struggling to acquire a work permit. Somehow, I embraced a deep-seated belief that my situation was unique and that I did not have to do what everyone else was doing. In my heart of hearts, I still found solace in the thought that in God's time, He would make all things beautiful.

The construction site was my predominant universe. There, I forged relationships with other contractors performing various jobs. Among them was a lady from Colombia who had a cleaning crew of girls. One of them, a girl from Peru, became an acquaintance of mine.

At lunch, or whenever we had opportunity, we would sit together and chat. During one of our encounters, I asked her if she had resolved the issue of her immigration status, to which she responded that she had not but had talked to someone at the construction site who supposedly had connections that could help. I asked if she could put me in touch with the intermediary; she had no problem with the request and hastily agreed. A few weeks later, when the individual showed up, she introduced him to me. Based on his story, his contact was a woman who worked for the immigration authorities. I was not sure whether to believe him or not but decided to follow up on the lead. He gave me a number to call, which I did. To my surprise, someone answered. I mentioned that a mutual acquaintance had given me her phone number in connection with immigration issues. She indicated that she could not talk over the phone but agreed to meet me at a nearby mall in the parking lot. At the appointed time, a car with government-issued license plates pulled up, and a Hispanic woman got out.

I had been waiting in the background, not knowing if I was about to fall for a ruse derailing my future. When she looked around and did not see anyone, she stood there waiting for a brief period, glancing at her watch from time to time. At that point, not perceiving any danger, I approached her and introduced myself to her in Spanish. She assured me she could help but that it was going to cost me $2,000 dollars. Her terms were that I would give her half the money up front and the rest when the deed was done. I was skeptical and started asking her probing questions. She indicated that she was not prepared to have that discussion and that the choice was entirely mine. I let her know that I needed time to think about it.

Before she left, she asked where I was from. When I told her my story, she seemed very eager to help, asking if I had ever thought about just getting married to resolve my immigration status once and for all. I responded that I only believed in marriage based on love. She looked at me skeptically and asked, "What other motivation could there be for marriage other than sincere love? You look like a nice young man with a bright future ahead of you. Why don't you find someone you like and settle down?" Before I could answer, she had started walking toward her car. I went home that day with a lot to think about.

Several weeks later, I called her again and asked if we could meet somewhere, as I had made up my mind to move forward with the initiative. We agreed to meet at her house. I gave her the $1,000 initial deposit, which had taken me months to save. She indicated that I would be hearing from her following a period of about three months.

I continued to work in construction, painting houses. I never complained; whatever I was asked to do, I did to the best of my ability. The patron considered me his most reliable worker. When other side jobs came up, he would ask me if I would consider working over the weekend. He would then pick me up and drive me to the job site, picking me up again at the end of the day. This way, I made extra money. As desperate as I was to establish myself, I did my best to honor and support my parents. At every opportunity, I would send them money. Mom would always take the time to write back and tell me how appreciative she was that I would choose to help them out. She assured me that I was in her prayers every day. I would read her letters and feel so encouraged to press on. I felt like I had found the motivation to work hard, that God was behind the scenes, molding something beautiful out of my apparent chaos.

One of the weekend jobs I remember doing was in Coral Gables at the patron's friend's house. The man lived in a beautiful mansion with his two daughters, who were both studying at the University of Miami. As I took a break from work, I approached one of the girls and asked her in Spanish if she was attending school. She responded that she was a student at the University of Miami. I then asked if she could walk me through the process of applying for admission. Before she could answer, I explained that I had graduated from a university in Cuba and was looking to enroll in graduate school. The girl turned out to be quite helpful. For the few days that I worked at their house, she showed me special attention, stopping by to ask if I needed anything to eat or drink. After hearing my story, she assured me that God was looking out for me and that I should stay focused on my goal. It seemed obvious to me that at every turn, God was selectively sending me people to bless and encourage me. At this point in my life, I quit feeling sorry for myself. My one and only goal was to persevere till the end. Whatever was in my sphere of influence, I resolved that I would do it to the best of my ability and God would take care of the rest. Knowing that my journey was not solely about me but also others whom the Lord was going to bless through me, gave me the hope that it was just a matter of time before things took on a different turn.

One of Miguel's friends who had a janitorial business came by the house one day. When Miguel introduced him to me, I asked if he had any extra work for me to do. Fortunately, he said that he could use my help. I started working with him at night, cleaning dry-cleaning shops across the city. We mopped floors, cleaned toilets, and did some light painting occasionally. We would work until past midnight sometimes, and in the morning, I would wake up to go to my regular daytime painting job. I found myself so tired much of the time, but I kept pushing myself. My prayer was always that God would preserve my health. If I ever got sick and needed to go to the hospital, that would not only be a blow to my health but a financial disaster. Without medical insurance, I didn't know what I would do.

CHAPTER 15
Roadblocks

Three months after my encounter with the lady who was supposedly working on my papers, I called her, only to hear the message that the number I called was disconnected. I tried to stay calm, rationalizing that people often changed numbers for whatever reason. My only other option was to go to her home, where I had been before to give her the initial deposit. When I arrived, I asked one of the neighbors about the folks who lived next door. The neighbor commented that as far as he could remember, the house had been vacated about a month prior and he had no idea where the owners moved to. It was a tough pill to swallow; I had just flushed $1,000 down the drain.

I went back to the intermediary for an explanation, but none was forthcoming. He felt sorry, but there was really nothing he could do. I asked him if he knew of any other contacts. He responded that he knew of a Mexican lady but did not have her phone number. I pressed him to get it for me. All he could say was that he would investigate further.

To my surprise, he showed up a few days later with the phone number, probably to make up for the previous loss. I called the lady almost immediately, and after I explained the purpose of my call, she asked if we could meet. We arranged to meet that same day in some location along the bus route. She turned out to be a woman who seemed to be in her early forties; she was very talkative and some-what easygoing. I explained to her my earlier experience, and the loss of a thousand dollars. She listened sympathetically and asked a few questions. In the end, she explained that had I contacted her in the immediate past three to six months, she would have been in a better position to help as there had been an amnesty program affecting farm workers. However, she said that if I were interested in marriage, she could talk to someone she knew who might be interested. We were back to square one by talking about marriage, a subject I had avoided for the longest.

"What if I don't like her, or she does not like me?" I asked her.

"You never know, *moreno*," she responded. At this point, she was comfortable enough to call me moreno, which was a nonderogatory term similar in meaning to *negro* in the Hispanic culture.

Out of the blue, I said to her, "If I can't marry the woman you have in mind, can I just marry you and get it over with?"

She laughed heartily. Standing up to make a point, she turned over to me and said, "Let me tell you something, moreno. I have never been with a black man before, and I don't intend to start now."

"Okay, maybe you don't know what you're missing," I retorted.

She looked at me in utter disbelief. Yelling, she asked, "Who are you, and how dare you talk to me like that?"

Looking at her straight in the eyes, with a surge of confidence, I said to her, "Watch me." Then I walked up close to her and kissed her on the cheek.

She blushed, saying in her confusion, "You are impossible. I don't think I have met a daring black man like you."

I responded in Spanish that I was a proud black man, and her confusion was even more palpable at this point.

"So you speak Spanish?" she asked.

I responded, "Better than you, and that is not meant to be an insult."

We carried on the rest of the conversation in Spanish, which led her to ask, "You are an African, but how come you speak Spanish?"

"Yes, I am, and why not?" I replied.

At this point, she was in my camp. Since it was getting late, she indicated that she had to leave but promised to call me as soon as she had the girl's number. If for whatever reason things did not work out, she said she was going to offer herself in marriage as a last resort. As if to assure me that she was serious, she hugged me and kissed me on my lips, giving me no time to react. She then walked away immediately. Now I was the one who was more confused.

I got home that evening, and as promised, she called to give me the girl's phone number. Not only did she provide the number, but she had already contacted the girl and explained my predicament, coaxing the girl to the point of leaving no stone unturned. We arranged to meet the following day; I gave her the address of where I lived, and she promised to pick me up the following day after 5:00 p.m. True to her word, she showed up as I waited in front of the house. I got in the car and directed her to the nearest park, where we sat and talked.

Her name was Lupe. After introducing ourselves to each other, I launched into my story right away, giving her background information about how I got to the US and what my plans and ambitions for the future were. I went on to explain that the only barrier standing in my way was not having authorization to work in the US.

She only asked one question after hearing my narrative. "Do you want to marry me just for the papers or for love?"

I explained that I was not able to falsely proclaim love and marriage at first sight, because I did not know who she was and, in fairness, she did not know me either. I went on to add that, in answer to her question, I wanted both but thought that getting to know each other first would be a good starting point. She agreed with me in principle and suggested that we meet again the following week. We continued to meet at least every week over a two-month period.

The time had come for me to leave Miguel's house. An older gentleman who was living by himself in a two-bedroom apartment in the area where I lived had put out an advertisement leasing one of the bedrooms. I called him as soon as I saw the advertisement. He offered to pick me up so I could look at the apartment when he found out that I did not have a car. I told him that I was ready to move in immediately. Miguel and his wife provided me with some of the basics I would need and helped me move my belongings. I could not thank them enough for what they had done for me; I prayed for the Lord's blessings upon them as often as I could. What they had done for me was much more than I could have ever imagined.

To date, whenever I think about them, I still grow profoundly emotional about the support they provided to a total stranger. Truth be told, while Miguel used to attend church services with his wife, he was not much of a religious individual, but he had the love of Christ, uncommon to many of us professing Christians. The love and sacrifice he showed me was simply overwhelming, to say the least. Not only was he used to channel the Lord's blessings upon me, but every subsequent blessing that would flow through me to others would go to his credit. I knew I could never repay him for what he did for me. As often as the Lord laid it upon my heart, my pledge was to pray, pray, and pray for him and his family.

Lupe and I continued to meet and talk until we both felt comfortable about the step we were about to take. I asked if her family would accept me into their Hispanic heritage. She responded that even if they did not, this was not about them. So we decided to go to the courthouse and solicit a marriage license. She had a friend who agreed to be our witness. To be able to walk out of the courthouse with the marriage license in my hand that day was another blessing out of God's bounty. From that day forward, my life was going to change forever.

During that same week, I went to the immigration office and picked up all the necessary forms I would need to file my petition as I could not afford a lawyer. I filled out all the forms myself and got the necessary affidavits, fingerprints, and so forth. Then I returned the application packet a few days later to the same office. Now it was just a matter of waiting for the response from the immigration authorities. I continued to do the painting job, but the housing project was almost coming to an end. The living arrangement proved challenging because Lupe and I lived some distance from each other and her moving into my shared apartment was not going to be possible. I could also not relocate to her area, as I did not have any means of transportation to get to work. She resorted to paying me a visit whenever she was able, mostly over the weekends.

My plan was to enroll in graduate school as soon as my immigration status changed. Having done a little research, my preference was ideally to attend the University of Florida in Gainesville, but leaving Miami at that time was not an option. The two local schools at my disposal were the University of Miami (UM) and Florida International University (FIU). UM was too expensive, and FIU seemed like the obvious choice. I got the application packet and started working on having my credentials from Cuba translated into English. I had studied metallurgical engineering in Cuba; for my master's degree, I thought a degree in mechanical engineering with an emphasis in materials would better augment design capabilities in my portfolio. I asked about financial aid programs and was told that there were several opportunities available. I followed up on all the leads, leaving no stone unturned.

In the meantime, I checked my mail almost every day. Eventually, the work permit arrived in the mail. It was a surreal moment. I thought about everything I had been through to get to this moment. It did not sink in; nothing felt different. The only difference was a piece of paper in my hands stating that I was authorized to work in the US. I told Lupe and a few of my friends about it, and that was the end of the story.

I had been out of school for more than two and half years by this time and did not really have any employment history. Finding a professional job was not going to be easy. I started making numerous applications but just could not land a job of my liking. That was why going back to school made a lot of sense. Besides, the economy was not doing very well. A case in point was an advertisement in the local paper for meter readers by the city government—no experience was required. I applied for the position and was called for an interview, but almost three thousand individuals had applied for the same position, and they only needed to fill five slots. At this point, I did not want to continue doing menial jobs; I wanted a meaningful full-time or part-time job that would allow me to attend school in the evening.

My next break occurred through my wife Lupe. She told me that she knew of a guy from Aruba who was heading a program called Outward Bound for high school kids. The program, funded by the Department of Education, was intended to provide disadvantaged kids with the opportunity to experience college life while they were still in high school. The program manager was looking for a math instructor and had mentioned it to Lupe in case she knew someone. When she approached me about it, I did not hesitate to probe the issue further. I spoke over the phone, informally, with the program manager, who asked that I show up at the Miami Dade Community College (MDCC) campus so that he could show me around. Meeting the manager was a breath of fresh air; he was smart and a very nice individual to be associated with. We bonded almost immediately. I figured out that being in this environment was going to be good for me intellectually and would allow me to meet other professionals who would in turn help me expand my network. To cut a long story short, he gave me the job. It was a part-time job, working only twenty hours a week.

Shortly after that, Lupe and I were given an appointment pertinent to the application for permanent residency. We were still living apart, due to the logistics which were still outside our control. We gathered all the evidence we could find and showed up for the appointment. They separated us and posed the same questions to each of us. Unfortunately, not all our answers matched. The interviewer later asked us to sit in front of his desk, where he notified us that he was going to deny our application because some of our answers on the most intimate details of our lives were too divergent. I attempted to explain to him our unique situation, but he was having none of it. He indicated that he was going to do a follow-up inquiry into the matter. We left that day and decided it was time to move in together, assuming that he was going to follow through with the investigation he had alluded to. I presumed that at the least, finding us in the same dwelling would work to our advantage.

We quickly found a two-bedroom apartment in the Kendall area in a very good neighborhood. It was a condo owned by a doctor working at a hospital in the same area. We moved in almost immediately. The old man I was sharing the apartment with was not happy that I was going to be leaving without sufficient notice. I understood his concerns but was not able to explain my situation any further. I agreed to give him a few hundred dollars for the inconvenience, and he appeared to be agreeable to that arrangement.

Lupe and I did our best to make the apartment feel like home. We had started our life together. The only drawback was that she had to drive a longer distance to get to work. To supplement our income, she suggested that we both enroll in the income tax classes sponsored by H&R block. Upon completion of the program, I worked with H&R block, doing taxes for the community. The lucky part was that Lupe had connections within the Mexican community in the southern part of Florida who needed help doing taxes. She brought many clients to my attention, and we used to charge them a flat fee of twenty dollars per tax return. Most of my friends had no idea how taxes were done and would approach me for help. We kept very busy during tax season. These were rays of hope that my life was slowly beginning to stabilize, but my impending goal was to get into graduate school, which was where all my energy was directed.

Not long after becoming part of the Upward Bound program at MDCC, I was given the opportunity to teach a few remedial math classes to regular college students. I had asked my boss in the Upward Bound program to introduce me to the dean of the mathematics department so I could teach a few classes in that department also. After reviewing my credentials and noting that I spoke Spanish, he hired me immediately and gave me the syllabus and textbooks. That was all I really needed. On my first day teaching, I introduced myself to the students as an adjunct mathematics instructor. I told them a little about myself and let them know how serious I was about their success. I also gave them my phone number and asked them to call me at home at any time of day or night if they ever needed math-related help. They were pleasantly surprised that an instructor would go out of his way to provide his personal phone number. I also indicated that I would be spending a few hours in the math lab every weekday and would be available for tutoring sessions.

We had gotten off to a good start; at least I could tell they were paying attention. Before delving into the lesson for the day, I asked them to write a paragraph explaining why they either liked or disliked math. Math had been my favorite subject ever since high school. I shared with them a few tricks they had never known before. I was so driven and motivated to impart knowledge and working with college students looked like a great opportunity as I prepared to go back to school myself. At the end of the first lesson, a few of them came around to chat with me. Some just wanted to introduce themselves and get to know me. There were, without a doubt, a few female students who might have had hidden agendas as they approached me, but I was quick to point out that I would maintain respectful, appropriate relationships with all my students.

When things began to settle into a routine, I realized that my work permit was, however, about to expire and I had not heard from the immigration authorities about my residency case. I asked Lupe if we could go to the immigration office to follow up. She took a day off from work, and we set off early in the morning to secure a place in the queue. When our turn came, we were ushered in to see an immigration officer, who asked the purpose of our visit. I explained to him that my application for permanent residency had been denied on a previous visit. I went on to explain that the officer attending our case had not provided an adequate explanation for the denial and therefore we were there to follow up on my case. I also told him that my work permit was about to expire and that I needed an extension, if possible. The attending immigration officer was rather sympathetic to our case this time around, as he started to review the file himself. He then told us that he did not see any anomalies with the file but needed to talk to the previous officer. In the meantime, he extended my work permit for another six months. I thanked him, and just before leaving, I mentioned to him that I was getting ready to enroll in graduate school and did not wish to miss another year. I asked if my residency permit would take longer than six months. He indicated that if there were no issues to follow up on, I would receive it in the mail no later than six months.

I got the permanent residence card in about three months following our second visit. God had come through for me in a mightier way than I could have imagined. After more than three years of being in the US, I was now a permanent resident. All I could do was thank my Father in Heaven for a major breakthrough in my life. It was just too good to be true.

Figure 17: MDCC in Miami where I taught Remedial Mathematics as an adjunct instructor (Courtesy of MDCC Picture Gallery)

Chapter 16
God's Goodness and Favor

Having received my permanent residence card, I was able to apply for admission to FIU for the spring intake starting in 1992, taking advantage of in-state tuition for legal residents. I also put in an application form for financial aid. In the meantime, I was really enjoying teaching at MDCC. I signed up to spend additional hours each day providing tutoring services to needy students in the math lab. I was paid an additional stipend for the hours I spent in the lab tutoring students. Merely being in an academic setting was quite a break from all the negatives I had been exposed to working in construction. I had seen the workers there engage in all sorts of vices, such as snorting cocaine, drinking on the job, and other behaviors that were not conducive to a healthy work environment.

I was heavily involved with the Upward Bound program with the high school kids about three times a week. As time went by, I was also given the opportunity to work with veterans returning to college. This was an extension grant of the Upward Bound program tailored specifically to veterans' needs. I provided teaching and tutoring services in remedial mathematics classes to prepare them for college. Given all these responsibilities, I was spending almost a full day at MDCC; I was getting accolades and recognition, forging great friendships. My evaluations at the end of every semester were overly positive. Students wrote very positive reviews about my unique methods of teaching. The head of the department, having noticed my accomplishments, gave me additional classes. I also had quite a few female admirers who would not take no for an answer. I established a good friendship with a student from Puerto Rico; our friendship was pure and fulfilling. Whenever she needed a shoulder to cry on, I was there for her but we both knew our bounds. We really enjoyed each other's company, to the extent that both of us were a bit apprehensive about the realm of possibilities downstream.

Given that all my students had my home phone number, some of them used to call home routinely to ask for help and, true to my word, I provided as much help as needed. On one occasion, one of the girls in my class called in the evening and asked for me, identifying herself as my student. My wife, who had answered the phone, asked her to state the reason for the call. She responded that she was stuck with her homework and needed help. Instead of giving me the phone, my wife simply hung up on the poor girl and then turned over to me in shouting mode, asking why all the "bitches" had to be calling home all the time. I tried to explain that it was my idea to have them call, but she was having none of it. She went on to say that from then on, none of them were ever to call home.

"Please explain to them in no uncertain terms how things are going to be going forward," she added.

I could not believe what I was hearing; this was my job, and I was just trying to help my students. I tried to avoid an argument by retiring to bed early that night. Several days later, someone from the math lab called home in the morning to ask if I would make myself available to help one of the students. When my wife picked up the phone, she insulted the lady, causing me profound embarrassment. I attempted to explain, but as usual, she was having none of it. She resorted to shouting and almost exercised physical violence. At this point, I knew that our marriage was on shaky ground. I had not seen this side of Lupe and was not sure how to deal with it. On another occasion, one of my female workmates in the math lab called home to ask for me, but when Lupe became rude, she returned the favor in kind. What ensued from that conversation was chaos of the highest order. The girl from the math lab said something to the effect that she could not understand how a smart guy like me would end up with such a woman. I was on my way to the lab when that conversation transpired; I got to hear about it when I arrived at work that day. My workmate in the lab apologized for the exchange, but the damage could not be undone.

Lupe had shown me her true colors, such that I understood she felt insecure. I tried to ignore all these distractions and kept my eye on the prize. At this point, my old friend McWale had been offered a scholarship to study for a PhD in South Carolina. Lupe and I drove from Miami all the way to South Carolina to meet him and his wife. One evening during our visit, we decided to go to a club just to pass time. Our friends invited another girl to join us, and we took turns to dance among ourselves. Lupe did not want to participate in the dancing. She sat there quietly, sipping a drink. At one point, I asked the other girl who had accompanied us to dance with me, with Lupe looking on. When Lupe saw us dancing, she got up and stood in between us. It was ridiculous and unbelievable. Now everyone in the club had noticed what was going on, and they were cheering. It was a chaotic scene to say the least. She turned over to me and let me know in no uncertain terms that we would be leaving for home that same night. My buddy McWale and his wife were equally embarrassed by this behavior. They chose to leave the club by taxi. It was about 2:00 a.m. when we set off, heading back to Miami. I was very sleepy driving at such a late hour. When it became apparent that I could not drive anymore, Lupe took over. We had to stop and sleep along the way when both of us could not continue driving. By the grace of God, we reached home safely. However, it was clear from that point onward that our marriage was unsustainable. All manner of respect had been lost, and it was all downhill from there.

I started the master's program in January of 1992. Fortunately, all my classes were in the evening, according me the opportunity to attend MDCC in the morning and then catch a bus to FIU in the late afternoon. I would then catch two buses after class, arriving home on a good day at around 11:00 p.m. at night. When I had assignments to grade, I would stay up till 1:00 or 2:00 a.m. before retiring to bed. For that reason, I had no problems sleeping, as I would often be too tired to stay awake. This became my routine for the duration of the master's program. Having been out of school for so long, it was a challenge to suddenly be exposed to multi-variable calculus and fluid mechanics.

The only way I was going to survive graduate school was by joining forces with classmates. With the passage of time, I found three trustworthy friends I could study with. One was a guy from Colombia, another from Puerto Rico and the other from Peru. Occasionally, I would also study with a Chinese student. As I got to know him more, I marveled at the depth of his intelligence. His level of preparation compared to the rest of us was simply unparalleled. However, it was the three trustworthy friends that I would mingle with the most. We bonded in good friendship and, rather than only studying together, we also got to visit each other's homes frequently. At the end of every semester, we would go to a favorite Latin American club known as Treasure Island and sip a few drinks whilst watching loosely clad dancing women. I recall one instance when my buddy from Colombia got so drunk that he told one of the girl dancers that he was madly in love with her as she joined us at the table for a drink. What a hilarious moment it was!

As we felt more comfortable with her, I ventured to ask why she chose the lifestyle of dancing in bars in front of men. I was stunned to learn that she was pursuing her bachelor's degree at one of the local schools and that the dancing was how she chose to pay for her studies and care for her ailing mother. From where she stood, she did not see this as an immoral lifestyle; it was simply a convenience driven by necessity. As we engaged her in further conversation, I soon discovered what a decent human being she was. I felt silly that I had been judgmental and unaccommodating. If there was any lesson for me in this encounter, it was that I should never judge a book by its cover.

As we advanced further into the master's program, classwork became so demanding that I needed to give up some of the classes I taught at MDCC to be able to cope, given that my studies were now a priority. I would wake up early in the morning, pack my lunch and dinner, and then head to MDCC. After a long day at MDCC, I would recalibrate my mindset and head to FIU for my evening classes. When I had pending assignments, I would go to FIU early in the afternoon to join my college mates. To make matters worse for me, I had to learn from scratch how to write programming code in Pascal or C/C+++. With Lupe's help, I had previously managed to buy a 286 computer, on which I did most of my programming assignments. To state that I was challenged to the nth degree was an understatement, but I put in all the effort I could muster, often staying up late into the night.

At home, my relationship with Lupe was not on the best of terms. We were now sleeping in separate bedrooms and saw each other very little. We only had one car, which she used to drive to work, and I, on the other hand, had to rely on public transportation, which was often unreliable. On rainy days, it took even longer to get home. There was at least one instance when I was not able to catch the last bus and ended up taking a bus going in the opposite direction to downtown, where I spent the night at the train station. I resisted calling Lupe to pick me up as it was so late. At this point in my life, I had been through so much that nothing really bothered me anymore. I was resolute in my faith that sooner or later, something would give.

Despite all the issues, I kept doing my best, taking it one day at a time. I kept reminding myself that the worst had passed and that only good days lay ahead of me. Life became a boring routine; I followed the same program almost every day. Every now and again, I made new friends who were also struggling with similar issues. Going to church over the weekend was the only refreshing activity that helped to break the monotony. Being in church on Sunday was a powerful reminder of God's goodness and faithfulness.

Just before the start of the fall semester in 1992, Hurricane Andrew swept across the South Florida area, leaving untold devastation. I had never experienced a hurricane before, so I was not sure what to expect. One of Lupe's cousins—a single mom with a ten-month-old baby at the time—had asked if she could spend the night with us at the apartment. Based on the projections, areas to the South were likely to get the brunt of the hurricane. Lupe tried to reach out to the rest of our family living in the Homestead area, but none of them thought it would be a big deal, so they preferred to stay put. Around 11:00 p.m, we started to experience strong winds from the hurricane. We put the baby to sleep and kept monitoring vulnerable locations of the apartment. Our apartment was on the second floor. It had a balcony with a screen, and the sliding door leading to the balcony kept shaking with every gust of the wind. I had to hold on to it from time to time to mitigate the shaking. The following morning, when it was safe to go outside, we stepped out to survey the damage. It then dawned on me that all my neighbors had experienced some form of damage. Our apartment was the only one in the entire building that escaped unharmed.

I was reminded of the biblical verse in Psalm 91: "A thousand may fall at thy side but it shall not come nigh thee…" The devastation around us was unbelievable. The city had been converted into what looked like a war zone overnight. My wife attempted to call her family members but to no avail; the phones were not working. She suggested driving over there, but I was not sure if it was safe to do so. She kept insisting, leaving me no choice. It was about twenty to twenty-five miles to get to the Homestead area. We tried using the highway, but it was blocked, so we had to try Krome Avenue instead. It took us almost six hours to get to the first home and probably another hour to get to the second one. They were all safe but had lost almost everything. They grabbed whatever they could and followed us home. There must have been close to twenty people in our apartment when we got back; every bit of floor space was utilized to accommodate everyone. The women got busy and prepared warm meals for everyone. We set up one bathroom for the ladies and the other for the men. There was nothing much to do except sit and wait until life returned to some semblance of normalcy.

I returned to work and school the following week, but life in South Florida was not the same again. I kept pushing myself, taking it one day at a time. A lot of students dropped out of school to attend to their impending needs emanating from the hurricane. Others took advantage of the economic opportunities and did very well for themselves. One of my mates in graduate school dropped out to help his father, who had much work to do in construction. The Colombian guy I had previously worked for in construction called me one day and asked if I would like to return and work for him again, promising to pay a lot more than before. I thanked him for the offer but politely let him know that I had moved on. Short-term gains were but mere distractions in my journey.

Figure 18: FIU in Miami where I attended Graduate
school (Courtesy of FIU Picture Gallery)

CHAPTER 17
Graduate School, Second Year

The year 1992 rolled into 1993, and the usual routine continued. Lupe and I reached a point where it made sense for both of us to move on. She came to the apartment one day and packed her belongings. I made no attempt to stop her. Before she left, she indicated that she had something to say. I sat down quietly and listened. She did not mince words; she spoke her mind. She started by saying that when she first met me, she thought I was different from other men she had met previously but that, over the years, she had come to realize that I was no different. She wanted me to know that she loved me but had reached the conclusion that the best thing for us to do was separate. All things considered, I thanked her for what she had done for me. I went on to say that if I ever became successful in life, I would always attribute that success entirely to her. I assured her that if she ever needed anything at all, I would always be there for her. When there was nothing more to be said, we both cried bitterly, not even sure why we were doing so. Perhaps it was the thought that this was going to be the last time that we would live together and that there were things we would miss about each other.

I was back to living alone again. I knew that as time went by, I would notice her absence acutely. It would be remiss of me not to mention that following that episode, I met a lady from Trinidad at MDCC; she had come to the math lab for help, and I had helped her several times. Her name was Bettie. One day she asked me if I liked cake, to which I said yes. To my surprise, she baked a cake over a weekend and delivered it to the math lab. Sharing a sweet tooth, we spontaneously became friends. She invited me to her home several times, where she lived with her sister, brother-in-law, and two children. Her cooking was extremely good. As a private tutor, I helped her with her homework occasionally but never asked her to pay me for the services. What I did not know is that she had fallen in love with me. I kind of sensed it, but I kept my cool; I was not ready for another relationship. One day, she could not contain herself. She asked if she could talk to me when I had a free moment, and most certainly, I had no objection. She did not mince words. She said it as plainly as she could. I did not want to hurt her feelings; all I said was that we should focus on friendship first and then maybe with time something could come out of it. This looked like a reasonable compromise, as we did manage to maintain our friendship. She was there for me whenever I needed her, helping to break the cycle of monotony.

I met other people who needed tutoring, most of whom became very good friends. Among them was a lady from Colombia. She would ask me to go to her house periodically to provide tutoring and in turn she would pay dearly for the services. After all, she was spending her millionaire boyfriend's money. Knowing my position, I thought she was only motivated by a desire to help me out. There was also another lady from the Dominican Republic, a dentist by profession. She too paid handsomely for my tutoring services. I took it that these were people the Lord had brought my way to bless me until the fulfillment of time.

The year 1993 then rolled into 1994. I completed all my classes at the end of 1993. The only thing left for me to do was complete my thesis. Sadly, my college mates who had been enrolled full-time graduated at the end of 1993. I was not deterred; I reminded myself that my situation was unique, therefore I was sticking to my game plan. I picked a thesis topic after consultations with several professors and decided to explore the world of smart materials. What I did not know was that there was not much in terms of available literature on the topic. This was a relatively novel idea, originating with the US Army. A smart structure was essentially one composed of an integrated network of sensors, actuators, and communication systems capable of sensing and responding to its environment in an intelligent fashion. Smart materials were gradually finding wide applications in the specialized industries, such as medical devices and other electronic industries. The goal of my project was to demonstrate on a laboratory scale how the combination of a sensor, actuator and control mechanism could be used as a single entity, to advance manufacturing solutions. The project was going to require a lot of programming work. I started off with literature searches for the first two months, trying to discern what had been published previously. I then designed an experimental model that would monitor incipient failure of a machining tool based on monitoring rapidly changing cutting forces. After discussing the model with my professor, we determined a budget for the experiments and started to lay the groundwork.

Now I was going to be spending a lot of time in the lab and would have little time for anything else. In the spring of 1994, after a long day at MDCC, I was heading to the lab when I spotted this gorgeous girl sitting by herself at the pond, watching the ducks as she waited for her class. I walked over to her and asked if we had met before. She responded that she did not think so. I then proceeded to introduce myself. She introduced herself as Joyce. After chatting for a while, I headed to the lab. The following day, she was at the same location, so I asked her if she sat there routinely while waiting for her class. Again, we chatted, this time a little longer. I found out that she was majoring in education and would be graduating the following spring. This time, we exchanged phone numbers and agreed to stay in touch.

Now I had something to look forward to on my way to the lab. She was not at the usual place all the time, but whenever she was, we would take a few moments to talk. As we got to know each other, I invited her to my apartment, and she invited me to hers. She loved to cook, and her food was so tasty. Physical exercise was a big part of her life; she exercised consistently and attended church service every Sabbath. As we became more comfortable with each other, she invited me to her church. I was happy to go with her and mentioned that I had attended the SDA church while I was in Cuba. She then introduced me to several of her friends in the church. Our friendship was growing stronger by the day. Unfortunately, we lived far apart; I lived in the south part of town, while she lived in the northeast section, and neither of us had a car. To get to her place, I would take a bus to the train station, a train downtown, and then another bus followed by a minibus.

I looked forward to seeing her. She was a down-to-earth individual—simple, very sweet, and caring. She was also tall and beautiful, with long dark hair almost reaching her waist. At 5' 9", she stood tall and imposing particularly in high heels. I could not quite figure out what her true racial identity was. Above all, she had a deep-seated love for God. Her happiest moments were always in the presence of other people. Laughter was a big part of her life. Being around her friends after Sabbath services was something she looked forward to. No one could deny the reality that a great friendship was developing between us. As we drew closer to each other, I related to her my prior situation with Lupe. From her perspective, she was quick to point out that she thought I had handled it very poorly. As a matter of fact, she scolded me for being so insensitive to a woman; she did not think I had been the victim but the instigator of the situation I had found myself in. For one, I was appreciative that she had an open mind and that she could speak without fear or favor. She had been through a breakup herself and felt vulnerable following this incident and was not looking to jump into another relationship just yet.

We talked a lot about the struggles we both had been through as part of the experience of living in this great country. We were both focused on school and looking forward to graduating, and both had student loans to worry about after graduation. I let her know up front that my goal was to graduate that December and that I was going to be very busy that year, working on my thesis. She understood and was quite supportive, occasionally going to my apartment out of her own initiative to prepare meals for me. At this point, I was very attached to her. We spoke over the phone almost every day.

I kept in touch with my parents as often as I could; I never forgot to care for their needs. I sent medication, money, and clothes for them, sometimes making great sacrifices in my budget to cater to their needs. I knew that my mother's health was not the best.

I remember getting a call at one point; it was my father calling as he asked me to hold on for my mother. She sounded so frail that I started to lose my calm. My dad had to get the phone from her to console me. He assured me that my aunt was getting her the best medical care they could find. We ended the conversation that day, but my thoughts were with her perpetually. I called Joyce to express my anxieties about my mom. She listened intently with profound empathy.

Several weeks later, on Mother's Day (May 14, 1994), I was awakened by the sound of a persistent ringing phone. As I looked at the phone, tears began to stream from my eyes down my cheeks. The phone kept ringing, and I made no effort to pick it up. It was mysterious how I got the premonition that what I had feared for so long had finally happened. Was this a self-fulfilling prophecy? I eventually picked up the phone but could not speak. My dad, on the other end of the line, kept on saying, "Hello? Hello? Hello?" He asked if I was there. I finally said yes in a shaky voice. He sensed that I was already crying and felt he did not have to explain any further. All he could say was that I should be strong. The time had come for my mother to rest from her suffering and the cares of this world.

A period of silence followed. I finally found the tone to let him know that I would be sending some money for the funeral arrangements. He repeated that I should stay strong. Then he eventually hung up. I felt as if air had just been sucked out of my chest. Alone in that apartment, I tried to search my memory for specific events that stood out. I remembered the last time I saw her. I remembered the hug she gave me, not to mention the prayer she said on my behalf. I remembered how difficult it was to part from her presence. It was too painful; I lost all appetite instantly. There was just nothing that could take away my pain. It was ironic and suffocatingly painful to lose my beloved mother on Mother's Day. I had earlier been thinking of going to church that morning to wish several mothers a happy Mother's Day, but mine was gone, and I was not even there for her.

The first person I called was Joyce. She immediately knew that something was wrong. Before I could even tell her, she asked if it was my mom and then said she was on her way. I then called my friend Kofi. He, too, indicated that he would be on his way. Next, I called my good friend and brother, Sichone, who was at the time living in LA. My other brother and friend McWale, who had attended graduate school in South Carolina, was now in Canada, doing his postdoctorate. I called him, too, to give him the sad news. This was the circle of my most trusted confidants. Since my arrival in the US, these were the friends I could trust with my life, and there was no doubt that they would be there for me. As I waited for Joyce to show up, I picked up my Bible and began to read scripture for comfort, but nothing could assuage the anguish that had pervaded my soul. Later, I picked up a pen and paper to write down a few memories about her.

Growing up, I was close to my mom. I loved her, and she loved me very dearly. She was my cheerleader. She infused confidence in my soul. She encouraged me to work hard. She taught me the value of faith in God and the importance of hard work. She had escorted me to secondary school when I was selected to attend Hillcrest Technical Secondary School. She gave me my first Bible. How does one return the favor when the focus of one's affection is gone? What was so painful was that I could not be there for her in her time of need. I knew I was not going to be there for her funeral because circumstances beyond my control did not permit.

Joyce was the first to arrive. I had left the apartment door open. She walked in and hugged me tightly. I could not contain my tears. She understood what I was going through and sat next to me without saying much. Later, she got up and started taking care of other chores around the apartment. She also started to prepare breakfast. My friend Kofi showed up eventually. The two of them took turns to pray. It was soothing to have them around in those dark moments. Kofi eventually left after a couple of hours, but Joyce stayed. We were not even dating; we were merely friends hanging out and being there for each other. After the many mistakes I had made in my life, I was determined this time around to take my time until I was sure I was being led in the direction of marriage with her.

The following day, I did not go to work or school. Joyce asked if I wanted her to stay with me, but I told her that she had done enough already and that I would be fine. I urged her to carry on with her day's activities. After she left, I called my good friend from Trinidad, Bettie, and asked if she could take me to the bank to send some money home. After hearing about the death of my mom, she showed up almost immediately. With her help, I sent the money and returned to my apartment to continue to mourn. By the end of the day, I had resigned myself to this fate, picked up the broken pieces, and was ready to move on, even though I knew it would be a while before life returned to normal.

Five days later, a good friend I attended church with heard about my grief and sent a card that brought so much peace to my broken soul. I read it over and over and found it applicable not just to my prevailing grief but practically to every area of my life. Based on the information on the card, the composer was unknown. It read as follows:

> Dear Abel,
>
> Our lives are but fine weavings
> That God and we prepare,
> Each life becomes a fabric planned
> And fashioned in His care.
> We may not always see just how
> The weavings intertwine,
> But we must trust the master's hand
> And follow His design,
> For He can view the pattern
> Upon the upper side,
> While we must look from underneath
> And trust in Him to guide.
> Sometimes a strand of sorrow
> Is added to His plan,
> And though it's difficult for us,
> We still must understand
> That it's He who fills the shuttle,
> It's He who knows what's best,
> So we must weave in patience

And leave to Him the rest.
Not till the loom is silent
And the shuttle ceases to fly
Shall God unroll the canvas
And explain the reason why
The dark threads are as needed
In the Weaver's skillful hand
As the threads of gold and silver
In the pattern He has planned.

CHAPTER 18
Last Stretch

I was in the last stretch; I needed to make my experiments work. I experimented with different algorithms, staying up late every night. I gave up some of my classes at MDCC so I could focus on my thesis. The work was challenging, and my professors very demanding. Spending over fourteen hours a day in the lab over the weekends was routine for me. I kept pushing and pushing, cognizant that every inch counted. I had no time for leisure activities. I was totally married to my work. Had it not been for Joyce stopping by from time to time to check up on me, I would have been a total recluse. As two semesters concluded, and we headed into the fall of 1994, I became aware that I did not have sufficient time at my disposal; there was still too much work left to be done. I wasn't sure how I was going to make it, but failure was certainly not an option. I worked harder than I had ever done in my entire academic life.

At the end of each experiment, I would take time to analyze the data to determine if it supported my hypothesis. It was not until November when I got my first big break. The data showed a pattern that made sense for the first time. I shared it with my professor, who agreed, but now demanded a lot more data. Over the subsequent few weeks, I did not know the light of day. I lived in the laboratory; on a few occasions, I slept there and went straight to MDCC when I needed to teach my classes. It was overwhelming, but there was no letting up at this point.

I completed my experiments well into December. Unfortunately, I had missed my deadline for graduation. Hoping for a break, I directed myself to the office in charge of graduation and asked for a special waiver to have my graduation backdated to December 1994. I was given a chance, but only on the condition that the submission of my thesis would occur by January 5, 1995. This meant that I had about two weeks to draft my thesis and have it reviewed and approved by January 5. I thanked the office of graduate studies for the opportunity and went to work. Schools had closed, fortunately, and therefore, I did not have to go to work. I worked on my thesis almost twenty hours every day and sometimes did not even find the time to eat.

When I look back at the support Joyce provided, I cannot help but think that she was another angel sent to help me in my time of need. While everyone around us was busy celebrating the holidays, she was there with me, helping me type my thesis. I would dictate to her what to write, and she would type. On New Year's Day, when everyone was celebrating the New Year, she was with me. At midnight, we paused for a few minutes to wish each other Happy New Year and then went right back to work. We completed the draft around 4:00 a.m. on January 1, 1995. In the dedication page, I invoked the memory of my dear mother, who unfortunately could not be there to see the final product but hopefully was looking down and beaming with motherly pride. Exhausted and with nothing else to give, we held hands and knelt in prayer to thank the God of heaven and earth, who had made it all possible.

On the morning of January 1, 1995, we were at Kinko's, making copies. I took a risk by making copies for the entire panel but reasoned that if the corrections were not major, I would have saved precious time. I located my professor the following day and asked him to review the draft. He gave me back the thesis draft with only minor comments; my gamble had paid off. All I needed to do was make additional copies for only the pages with comments. Again, Joyce was there for me. I circulated copies to the panel members on the deadline date. I also provided a copy to the office of graduate studies. The thesis defense date was scheduled for the following week. It was the first time in a long time that I found myself free and with nothing to do; it felt so weird.

On the designated day, I put on the only suit I had and headed to school using public transportation. Joyce had wanted to be there, but I asked her not to show up. We would celebrate the accomplishment later. My classmate from Colombia who was, at that time, doing his PhD was there with me. Following the formalities, they gave me about forty-five minutes to present the thesis. A question-and-answer session followed for another twenty minutes. I was nervous at the start but felt more comfortable as I delved further into the presentation.

Finally, I was a free man. I had graduated with a master of science degree in mechanical engineering, and my "Tropicana" was no longer a pipe dream. I looked for Joyce and gave her the good news. It was a joyous occasion for both of us; the relief I felt was surreal. I paused to wonder why my journey had been so long compared to that of my many peers and colleagues along the way. I did not have any easy answers, but I chose to think that this was the Lord's way based on my unique circumstances and experiences. Perhaps this was His way of wanting me to appreciate not just the destination but the process of learning to lean on Him. By taking me on the long, narrow, and winding path, it was His way of ensuring that I did not stray from my destiny due to my disobedience. Along this journey, I witnessed the Lord's goodness first-hand. I also saw that the Lord can do far more than we can ever think or imagine, if only we have faith even as tiny as that of a grain of mustard.

In short, He is the God of the impossible. Perhaps most important of all, I learned to trust him completely. In the end, maybe that was just my destiny, or maybe it was a test of faith and patience for the opportune moment. A colleague of mine with whom I shared my story could not have expressed it better when he said, "Every experience you went through was just another chapter in your book." Whatever the lesson, however long the journey, whatever the heartache, deep in my heart, I knew I had found a partner in Joyce.

CHAPTER 19
Final Thoughts

Following graduation, I was offered the chance to pursue studies in a PhD program, but I could not afford to be in school any longer while a host of family members looked up to me for support. The events that followed my graduation were even more meaningful in terms of validating what I believed to be the hand of Providence at work in my life. It was as if the faucet of God's blessings upon my life was turned on to flow unobstructed. This is material I hope to cover in the next tome of this book series. Suffice to say, for now, following graduation, I landed a job working at a firm making a variety of mechanical parts using the investment casting process. My background in materials proved relevant in that regard. From there, I went on to work at a medical device company making pacemakers and leads. Several years later, I moved to Dallas, where I worked for another medical device company making breast prostheses. I then moved to Houston (the city I now call home) to work for Guidant, another medical device company, accompanied by my wife-to-be, Joyce, who was at the time still based in Miami, attending graduate school and working as a teacher. Moving to Houston to work for Guidant turned out to be the best career move of my life.

Joyce and I had been dating for almost six years; she had been my support, pillar of strength, and confidant. I had searched my soul and found out that she was truly the only woman I could think of sharing my life with. I took a trip to Miami one weekend, carrying a special delivery. She was waiting for me in her apartment when I arrived. Unexpectedly, I knelt as she lay on the bed, and first of all, I thanked her for believing in me and sticking with me through thick and thin, even though I had nothing material to offer her when we first met. I thanked her for the many bus trips she had taken to see and support me and, above all, for being there for me when my mother passed away and for helping me with my thesis work, thus facilitating my graduation as planned. I then reached into my pocket to open the little box I was carrying. I asked her to marry me if she felt the same way about me so we could continue the journey together, hopefully for the rest of our lives.

On April 4, 1999, we flew to Las Vegas, where we got married in a simple ceremony, accompanied by several friends of mine and family members from her side. Our journey together had begun. In October of 1999, we moved into our first home, confirmation of the promise of our piece of the American Dream. At this point in my life, I could safely say that the "Tropicana" of my dreams had become a reality. In the year 2000, we both became citizens of the United States of America. Like many immigrants living in the diaspora, this great land has given us more than we ever thought possible. I do not pretend to have integrated the ranks of the rich and famous, but waking up every day and having the ability to do honest work that impacts patients' lives is a blessing I am truly thankful for. In the end, it dawned on me that my "Tropicana" was not about chasing a futuristic and abstract concept; it was about treasuring every seemingly miniscule blessing from above in the present.

Having been in the employ of Guidant corporation for seven years, the need to shut down the business unit I was part of inevitably presented itself, as the technology we had worked on was rendered less viable in the face of emerging drug-eluting stent technologies for cardiovascular applications. In response, God simply moved another pawn, opening another door and leading me to work for another medical device company in the Houston area, where I have continued to work as of the time of writing this book. The satisfaction I derive from working on technologies that directly impact human lives is the impetus that keeps me motivated every day.

As I look back to August of 1988, when I first arrived in Miami with only $450 in my pocket, without even knowing where I was going to spend my first night, everything pales in comparison to what the Lord has done for me since then. In the face of countless blessings from above, I can only say "Lesa wa maka," "El señor es todo poderoso," "God is great." From the depths of my soul, I dare to declare, "May everything that has breath praise Him. May all praise, glory, honor, and majesty be ascribed to Him and Him alone through all ages to come for all of His goodness and ever-abiding faithfulness."

This has been my journey across two continents and an island, a journey interspersed with failures and successes, sorrows and laughter, darkness and hope, need and abundance. But Christ has been the sole constant, and His grace has been sufficient for all my needs. In the face of adversity, God's love still abounds, and the best part is that the journey continues. Over the years, as I have had the chance to reflect and ponder the meaning and purpose of my life, I have asked myself what I could possibly give to my Creator as a token of my appreciation for all He has done for me. I have surmised that nothing short of my heart would be a worthy sacrifice. To this end, wanting to express my dedication to the mission He called me to, I felt compelled to write (on my fiftieth birthday) what I understood to be the purpose for my existence—a personal mission statement, if you will, that captures the essence and direction of my mortal life. This has been the motivation that propels me through life every day as I continue my life's journey. It is my hope and prayer that the reader will find inspiration in the thoughts summarized in the text below:

> I exist to do the will of my Father in heaven. I am a vessel unto His honor and an instrument of His righteousness. Having been formed in God's own image, I am wholly equipped mentally, physically, and emotionally to do all things through Christ, who strengthens me. I am alive today because there is a unique purpose the Lord would have accomplished through me and only me.

> By the grace of the Lord Jesus Christ and the power of the Holy Spirit, I will strive to elevate my Maker above all my labors and maintain myself unspotted from the lust of the eyes, the

lust of the flesh, and the pride of life in all forms and manifestations. Where I fall short, may I be reminded that God's grace abounds in my favor.

All that I am and possess today I received by grace for the glory and honor of His name. I will, therefore, use my gifts and talents for the extension of God's kingdom and in the service of humanity.

I will learn to be content with the Lord's blessings for my life, and I will honor Him with my substance and increase for as long as He lends me breath. Yet if in His wisdom, He should choose to take away what He has bestowed, may I still find the strength and courage to offer sacrifices of praise at His altar.

Amid life's toils and snares, may I be granted the wisdom to discern right from wrong and the will to pursue righteousness with all my strength, might, and soul. In all my undertakings, may I always seek God's perspective, no matter the cost. May I be rescued from the apathy of mediocrity, the abuse of power, and the false convenience of seeking man's approval rather than that of my Creator. Above all, may I never doubt my Maker's infinite wisdom but only rest by faith in His unchanging promises day by day.

Finally, in the pursuit of life's meaning and purpose, may I be endowed with the wisdom to recognize that the true measure of success consists not in the endeavor directed at accruing earthly gains but rather in the strength of character disposed unconditionally to obeying God's commandments and in being a channel of blessing in the welfare of mankind.

So help me, God, appreciate life's beauty in simplicity, stay true to my inimitable calling, and align my will with Thine for all eternity.

Appendix

Spanish Speech Text in Commemoration of Zambia's Twentieth Independence Anniversary

Compañeros de la Presidencia,

Compañeros y compañeras que nos honran con su presencia en este acto;

Nos complace reunirnos junto a ustedes en esta fecha para conmemorar otro aniversario más de la independencia de nuestra patria Zambia. Hace hoy exactamente veinte años que nuestro pueblo alcanzó la victoria a derrocar en 1964 el régimen británico tras una ardua y prolongada lucha armada y por primera vez estableció un gobierno a favor de los intereses populares. Este acontecimiento trascendental propinó un duro golpe a las fuerzas imperialistas y nos colocó en el seno del mundo progresista como nuevos aliados en la causa común por la liberación y el progreso del mundo.

Constituyó para nosotros un señalado honor qué sobre la importancia de este hecho ahora somos capaces de forjar nuestro destino según nuestros propios intereses.

Compañeros, solo es la historia auténtica de un pueblo qué puede reflejar correctamente su origen, el largo camino recorrido y en estado en que se encuentre. No fue coincidencia que las masas en nuestro país emprendieran la lucha anticolonial con la determinación más resuelta para alcanzar la libertad. No sería inútil desde luego, recordar este camino largo y difícil recorrido por nuestro pueblo en la lucha por conquistar la plena emancipación desde los primeros años del colonialismo inglés siempre defendiendo su derecho a la autodeterminación; motivados solo por el digno deseo de lograr la justicia social, la dignidad del hombre y sobre todo, liberar la nación del yugo colonial y abrir un camino hacia una vida mejor para las masas. Esta lucha se emprende tan pronto como en 1924 cuando el país se convirtió en un protectorado británico administrado primero por la British South African Company y después por el Ministerio de Colonias con el fin de poder controlar arbitrariamente los recursos humanos y naturales de nuestra patria.

Desde luego las fuerzas que unieron al pueblo zambiano en la lucha por la independencia fueron una consecuencia directa de muchos años de opresión colonial, un sistema de gobierno que negara a los zambianos los derechos y privilegios humanos en su propia patria.

La guerra de liberación se inició cuando un pequeño grupo de valientes mal armados se lanzó por asalto contra un puesto administrativo del colonialismo inglés. Sobre la base de este acontecimiento aparentemente insignificante, se abrió el camino hacia un largo y rico periodo de luchas populares contra los agresores.

Previo a desencadenamiento de esta decisiva etapa en la historia del país, había sido fundado el Congreso Nacional de Rhodesia bajo el lema: "El derecho a sufragio para todos." Sin embargo, las luchas emprendidas, concluyeron en la frustración de las aspiraciones del pueblo cuando la política federativa vinculó a Zambia, Zimbabwe y Malawi en un complejo político económico y ésta sentó las bases para las inversiones en gran escala de los monopolios anglo-americanos, parte de cuyos mecanismos aún mantienen hoy cierta vigencia.

Restituir la individualidad política y geográfica de nuestro país fue motor de la prolongada lucha que evolucionó adquiriendo mayor impulso cada vez. Con la formación del Congreso Nacional Africano de Rhodesia, se creyó un nuevo espíritu revolucionario que hizo hincapié en la necesidad de una acción resuelta para liberar al país junto con su pueblo y para ella utilizar todas las fuerzas de la lucha incluida la armada.

Cuando el partido ZANC fue prohibido, surgieron espontáneamente una serie de partidos políticos y mediante su fusión se formó finalmente el partido Unido de la independencia Nacional de Zambia encabezado por el presidente Kenneth Kaunda. Bajo este partido vanguardia, nuestro pueblo desarrollo el combate contra el poder colonial extendiendo el movimiento guerrillero a varias provincias de forma incontenible.

A un alto precio de sangre y sacrificio el país se coronó en victoria el 24 de octubre de 1964, fecha en que se proclamó la independencia del yugo colonial bajo el nombre: Republica de Zambia, siendo Kenneth Kaunda elegido para ocupar la presidencia de la nación. De esta forma se inició un proceso de transformaciones socioeconómicas.

Compañeros corresponde destacar qué es colonialismo era un sistema para sub desarrollar no solo a nuestro país sino a toda África y sin duda, el atraso económico por el cual atravesamos hoy en día es una herencia directa del periodo del desarrollo colonial. Este sistema de hecho significó para nuestro pueblo una pérdida de todo derecho humano y abrió el camino hacia la dependencia económica de la metrópoli.

Mientras los colonos se beneficiaban de la mayor parte de la riqueza nacional, nuestro pueblo era el último en su propia patria. El sistema educacional sólo existía para nuestro propio subdesarrollo ya que, no siendo derivado del medio zambiano, inculcaba en los jóvenes un espíritu de preferencia hacia todo lo corrupto y lo capitalista, dando lugar al desarrollo del subdesarrollo. El racismo por otro lado en su forma más drástica pretendía confirmar en la práctica la tesis sobre la desigualdad de las razas humanas. A nuestro pueblo le impusieron un sistema inhumano y antidemocrático de relaciones mutuas entre las razas según el cual los blancos constituían la élite y los africanos privados de los derechos políticos y sometidos a una cruel explotación. Gracias al mundo progresista, nuestra lucha encontró profundas simpatías y extensa solidaridad.

Compañeros las tareas a las que hemos tenido que hacer frente desde la consecución de la independencia nacional son inmensas y se dirigen hacia la restructuración de los modelos de desarrollo impuesto en el período anticolonial las cuales no responden a los intereses nacionales. A pesar de que no podemos avanzar con toda la rapidez que deseamos y necesitamos, saludamos este aniversario con muchos logros en las distintas esferas de la vida social.

En los esfuerzos por erradicar la ignorancia, el Ministerio de Educación lleva al cabo uno de los programas de expansión más ambicioso visto en el continente africano. Según cifras oficiales existen actualmente casi 3000 centros de enseñanza primaria (con una matrícula de más de un millón de estudiantes), casi 200 centros de enseñanza secundaria y varios de enseñanza superior, escuelas de comercio y técnico, escuelas de formación de maestros etcétera, en el servicio de una población de 5 millones de habitantes. Es de mencionar que ahora cada municipio cuenta por lo menos con una escuela secundaria lo que antes era privilegio de los centros urbanos de mayor concentración poblacional. Además, se trabaja por alcanzar la meta de un noveno grado como enseñanza básica para toda la población y se pone énfasis especial en la inclusión de carreras técnicas en el programa educacional.

Contamos con un sistema gratuito de atención médica existiendo actualmente más de 100 hospitales, 17 leprosorios, más de 600 centros asistenciales clínicas esparcidos por todo el país. La medicina preventiva ha recibido un considerable impulso, como resultado del cuál, la viruela ha sido erradicada. Se desarrolla una amplia campaña profiláctica para controlar varias enfermedades endémicas entre ellas malaria, tuberculosis y lepra.

En la esfera económica los logros alcanzados son espectaculares a pesar de las dificultades que enfrenta el país. Citamos como ejemplo la declaración unilateral de la independencia por el régimen de Ian Smith en Rhodesia del sur (Zimbabwe) que causó una considerable destrucción a nuestras rutas de comercio y agudizó nuestra posición desventajada como país sin costa pero fue un estímulo a los esfuerzos de la nación hacia la diversificación y la reorientación del comercio y a poner fin a la dependencia económica de Rhodesia y Sudáfrica.

El desarrollo económico se lleva a cabo según el plan quinquenal. En el primero, se hizo hincapié en la industrialización del país y como resultado fueron construidas una fábrica de cemento con una capacidad de 500 mil toneladas anuales, una planta hidroeléctrica con una producción anual de 5 mil millones de KW. Además, comenzó a funcionar la mina de Mamba sustituyendo la que estaba ubicada en Rhodesia como principal proveedora de coque y carbón.

En los 15 años siguientes se ha visto la construcción de la planta de fertilizantes con una producción anual hasta 200 mil toneladas, la refinería de petróleo que aparte de satisfacer las demandas internas, permite al país exportar sus restantes de refinales. También se construyó una segunda planta energética (por lo que al país no le es necesario importar este renglón), la fábrica de textiles y otros más de vital importancia para la economía nacional.

Un paso de importancia en cuanto al logro de la emancipación total del país ha sido la introducción de la política de Zambianización con el objetivo de sustituir los expatriados en la economía nacional. El comercio mayorista tradicionalmente en manos de la minoría asiática está actualmente reservado por ley a los zambianos. El estado refuerza a ritmo cada vez mayor, participación en la economía nacional controlando actualmente más de 61 por ciento de las acciones minerales y otras industrias de importancia. Esperamos que el poder este en el pueblo directamente mediante una democracia de participación industrial basados en cooperativas y bajo el control de dos trabajadores.

Compañeros, aunque hayamos logrado la Liberación Nacional, no pretendemos haber alcanzado la última meta. Reconocemos las dificultades económicas y los problemas sociales no resueltos que enfrentamos debido a la práctica actual del neocolonialismo, un sistema de explotación que crea obstáculos en nuestro camino hacia la auténtica independencia. Los neocolonialistas nos imponen modelos de desarrollo que conducen a la dependencia tecnológica, les proporcionan las principales ventajas y obstaculizan la solución de nuestros problemas. A través de los canales del sistema de pagos internacionales, descargan sobre nuestros hombros, el pago du su propia inflación, aumentando los precios de los artículos industriales que ellos exportan y reduciéndoles artificialmente para nuestras exportaciones dando lugar a una situación triste: la deuda externa impagable.

Nuestra lucha es por la total soberanía y los intentos de reestructurar las relaciones económicas con los estados capitalistas sobre bases equitativas y justas. Nos pronunciamos totalmente por la política de cancelación de la deuda externa y por el establecimiento de un nuevo orden económico ya que una estable economía mundial en fin de cuentas beneficia a todos los estados. Creemos desde luego que solo es bajo tal ambiente que los 4 mil millones de familias humanas tienen la posibilidad real de llevar a cabo una vida digna de autoabastecimiento.

Cómo joven estado realizamos consecuentemente en nuestras relaciones con muchos países del mundo una política de amistad orientada hacia la amplia cooperación y el apoyo. Las proporciones de esta cooperación se han ampliado considerablemente en los últimos años con los países del campo socialista y abarcan cada vez más nuevas esferas de la vida económica sociopolítica y cultural.

Desde temprano el apoyo de los pueblos que luchan por su liberación del colonialismo ha sido una de las orientaciones fundamentales de nuestra política exterior. Brindamos el más enérgico y resuelto respaldo a la SWAPO de Namibia Y el ANC de Sudáfrica cómo lo hicimos al movimiento popular por la liberación de Angola durante su lucha anticolonial, el FRELIMO de Mozambique y el Frente Popular de Zimbabwe. Constituye una anomalía la actual situación de Namibia y Sudáfrica donde el colonialismo y el racismo se oponen a un proceso lógico; la culminación de la lucha de liberación nacional africana.

Integramos como miembro activo entre otras organizaciones, los países de la línea del frente la OUA, el movimiento de los países no alineados y por principios apoyamos la consolidación de la economía nacional de cada país, la liberación de la explotación capitalista y de la dependencia neocolonialista. Reforzamos la soberanía de todos los países del derecho de elegir libremente la orientación del desarrollo nacional y apoyamos la lucha por liquidar la desigualdad de derecho en las relaciones internacionales.

Condenamos enérgicamente la carrera armamentista en virtud de la dependencia directa del desarme y el desarrollo. Los recursos para fines militares son tan necesarios para liquidar el atraso económico, el hambre y la miseria. Por causa de la misma, se nos privan de aquellos medios adicionales que nos podría conceder en concepto de ayuda si se lograra un acuerdo sobre la reducción de los gastos militares.

Es saludo a este aniversario, nosotros los jóvenes zambianos, tomamos la tarea de hacer nuestro, los ideales de los que alumbraron nuestro camino, luchar sin descansar contra las maquinaciones imperialistas, por la plena emancipación y bienestar total de nuestro pueblo. Como dijera el compañero Fidel Castro: "Sabremos cumplir del deber qué de nosotros demanda la hora actual y el porvenir de nuestro pueblo."

¡Viva la independencia de Zambia!

¡Viva el internacionalismo proletario!

¡Viva el ejemplo de Cuba!

¡Patria o muerte, Venceremos!

///

English Speech Text in Commemoration of Zambia's Twentieth Independence Anniversary

Distinguished comrades at the podium,

Comrades honoring us with your presence at this event;

We are pleased to meet with you on this date to commemorate yet another anniversary of the independence of our homeland Zambia. Exactly twenty years ago today, our people achieved victory in overthrowing the British regime in 1964 after a long and arduous armed struggle and for the first time established a government in favor of popular interests. This momentous event dealt a severe blow to the imperialist forces and placed us within the progressive world as new allies in the common cause for the liberation and progress of the world.

It was a remarkable honor for us that on the importance of this event we are now able to shape our destiny based on our own interests.

Friends, it is only the authentic history of a nation that can correctly reflect its origin, the long road traveled and the actual conditions it constitutes. It was no coincidence that the masses in our country undertook the anti-colonial struggle with the most resolute determination to achieve freedom. It would not be inconsequential, of course, remembering this long and difficult path traveled by our people in the struggle to achieve full emancipation from the first years of English colonialism, always defending their right to self-determination; motivated only by the worthy desire to achieve social justice, the dignity of man and above all, liberate the nation from the colonial yoke thus opening a path to a better life for the masses. This fight started as early as 1924 when the country became a British protectorate, administered first by the British South African Company and later by the Ministry of Colonies in order to arbitrarily control the human and natural resources of our homeland.

Of course, the forces that united the Zambian people in the struggle for independence were a direct consequence of many years of colonial oppression, a system of government that denied Zambians their natural human rights and privileges in their own homeland.

The liberation war began when a small group of brave, scantly armed men launched an assault on an administrative post of English colonialism. On the basis of this apparently insignificant event, the door was opened for a long and dignified period of popular struggles against the aggressors.

Prior to unleashing this decisive phase in the country's history, the Rhodesian National Congress had been founded under the motto: "One Man, One Vote." However, the struggles that were waged ended in the frustration of the people's aspirations when federal policy linked Zambia, Zimbabwe and Malawi in an economic political complex and this laid the foundation for large-scale investments by Anglo-American monopolies, part of whose mechanisms are still in force today.

Restoring the political and geographical individuality of our country was the engine of the long struggle that evolved, acquiring more and more momentum with the lapse of time. With the formation of the Rhodesian African National Congress, a new revolutionary spirit was created that emphasized the need for resolute action to liberate the country together with its people and for that reason to use all necessary force in the struggle including armed resistance.

When the ZANC party was banned, several other political parties sprang up spontaneously, and through their merger the United National Independence Party, led by President Kenneth Kaunda, was finally formed. Under this vanguard party, our people executed the fight against the colonial power by spreading the guerrilla movement to various provinces in an irrepressible way.

At a high cost of blood and treasure, the country was crowned in victory on October 24, 1964, the date on which independence from the colonial yoke was proclaimed under the name: Republic of Zambia, with Kenneth Kaunda being elected to occupy the presidency of the nation. In this way, a process of socio-economic transformations began.

Comrades, it is worth highlighting what colonialism was, a system for under-development not only of our country but also all of Africa, and without a doubt, the economic crises that we face today are a direct inheritance from the period of colonial development. This system in fact meant for our people a loss of all human rights and opened the way to economic dependence on the metropolis.

While the colonists benefited from most of the national wealth, our people were the last in their own homeland. The educational system only existed for our own underdevelopment since, not being derived from the Zambian milieu, it instilled in the youth a spirit of preference toward everything Western and corrupt, opening the way to the development of underdevelopment. Racism on the other hand in its most drastic form was intended to confirm in practice the thesis about the inequality of the human races. They imposed on our people an inhumane and undemocratic system of mutual relations between races whereby whites were the elite and Africans deprived of all political rights while subjected to cruel exploitation. Thanks to the progressive world, our struggle found deep sympathy and extensive solidarity.

Comrades, the tasks that we have had to face since the achievement of national independence are immense and are directed toward the restructuring of the development models imposed in the anti-colonial period, which do not appropriately respond to our national interests. Although we cannot move forward as quickly as we wish and need to, we celebrate this anniversary with many achievements in the various spheres of social life.

In efforts to eradicate ignorance, the Ministry of Education carries out one of the most ambitious expansion programs seen on the African continent. According to official figures, there are currently almost three thousand primary schools (with an enrollment of more than one million students), almost two hundred secondary and several higher education centers, business and technical schools, teacher training schools, among others in the service of a population of about 5 million inhabitants. It is worth mentioning that now each municipality has at least one secondary school, which was previously the privilege of the urban centers with the highest population concentration. In addition, efforts are made to achieve the goal of a ninth grade as basic education for the entire population and special emphasis is placed on the inclusion of technical careers in the educational program.

We have a free health care system, with currently more than one hundred hospitals, seventeen leprosaria, and more than six hundred clinical health centers scattered throughout the country. Preventive medicine has received a considerable boost, as a result of which, smallpox has been eradicated. A comprehensive prophylactic campaign is underway to control various endemic diseases including malaria, tuberculosis and leprosy.

In the economic sphere, the achievements made are impressive despite the difficulties facing the nation. We cite as an example the unilateral declaration of independence by the Ian Smith regime in Southern Rhodesia (Zimbabwe) that caused considerable destruction to our trade routes; sharpening our disadvantaged position as a landlocked country but was a stimulus to the efforts of the nation toward diversification and reorientation of trade while ending economic dependency on Rhodesia and South Africa.

Economic development is carried out based on a five-year plan. In the first, emphasis was placed on the industrialization of the country and as a result, a cement factory with a capacity of five hundred thousand tons per year, a hydroelectric plant with an annual production of five billion KW was built. In addition, the Maamba mine began operating, replacing the one located in Rhodesia as the main supplier of coke and coal.

In the following fifteen years, the construction of a fertilizer plant with an annual production of up to two hundred thousand tons was completed, an oil refinery which, apart from satisfying internal demands, allows the country to export its remaining refineries. A second energy plant was also built (so that the country does not need to import this line), the textile factory and others of vital importance to the national economy.

An important step toward achievement of total emancipation of the country has been the introduction of the Zambianization policy with the aim of replacing expatriates in the national economy. Wholesale trade traditionally held by the Asian minority is currently reserved by law for Zambians only. The state is steadily increasing its share of the national economy, currently controlling more than 61 percent of mineral stocks and other major industries. It is our hope that power will rest with the people directly through an industrial participation democracy based on cooperatives and under control of the workers.

Comrades, although we have achieved National Liberation, we do not claim to have reached the ultimate goal. We recognize the economic difficulties and unresolved social problems that we face due to the current practice of neocolonialism, a system of exploitation that creates obstacles on our way to true independence. Neocolonialists impose development models on us that lead to technological dependency, provide them with the main advantages and hinder the solution to our problems. Through the channels of the international payment system, they discharge on our shoulders, the payment of their own inflation, increasing the prices of the industrial items they export and artificially reducing them for our exports, giving rise to a sad outcome: the unpayable external debt.

Our fight is for total sovereignty and attempts to restructure economic relations with western states on an equitable and fair basis. We fully support the policy of canceling the external debt and the establishment of a new economic order, since a stable world economy ultimately benefits all states. We believe, of course, that it is only under such an environment that the 4 billion human families have the real possibility of leading a life worthy of self-sufficiency.

As a young state, we consistently carry out in our relations with many countries of the world a policy of friendship oriented toward broad cooperation and support. The proportions of this cooperation have expanded considerably in recent years with the countries of the socialist camp and increasingly encompass new spheres of socio-political and cultural economic life.

From early on, supporting the people fighting for their liberation from colonialism has been one of the fundamental orientations of our foreign policy. We offer the most energetic and resolute support to the SWAPO of Namibia and the ANC of South Africa, as we did to the Popular Movement for the Liberation of Angola during its anti-colonial struggle, the FRELIMO of Mozambique and the Popular Front of Zimbabwe. The current situation in Namibia and South Africa where colonialism and racism oppose a logical process, that is, the culmination of the African national liberation struggle, constitutes an anomaly.

We integrate, as an active member among other organizations, the frontline countries, the Organization for African Unity (OUA), the movement of the non-aligned countries and by principle; we support the consolidation of the national economy of each country, the liberation from Western exploitation and from neocolonialist dependency. We reinforce the sovereignty of all countries of the right to freely choose the orientation of national development and support the fight to eliminate inequality of law in international relations.

We strongly condemn the arms race by virtue of the direct relationship between disarmament and development. Resources for military purposes are so necessary to liquidate economic backwardness, hunger and misery. Because of this, we are deprived of any additional means that could be granted to us as aid if an agreement were reached on the reduction of military spending.

In honor of this anniversary, we the Zambian youth take on the task of making our own, the ideals of those who lit our way, fighting without rest against the imperialist machinations, for the full emancipation and total well-being of our people. As comrade Fidel Castro would say, "We will know how to fulfill our duty, which of us demands the current hour and the future of our people."

Long live the independence of Zambia!

Long live proletarian internationalism!

Long live the Cuban example!

Homeland or death, we shall overcome!

Spanish Speech Text in Commemoration of the Twenty-First Anniversary of the Founding of the OAU

Compañeros de la Presidencia,

Compañeros y compañeras asistentes a este acto.

Nos hace sentir privilegiados reunirnos junto a ustedes en esta tierra de Martí y Fidel para conmemorar otro aniversario más de la Fundación de la OUA y así reafirmar los lazos de amistad y hermandad que nos une. Un día como hoy en el año 1963 se dieron cita los grandes estadistas africanos en la admirada capital de Etiopia, Addis Ababa para fundar la organización de la Unidad Africana (OUA).

Este constituyó un hecho de gran trascendencia histórica para la lucha protagonizadas por los pueblos africanos contra la más criminal y vandálica opresión y explotación colonialista. Fue ahí donde se trazó el programa de acción con el esfuerzo de todos los pueblos africanos en el decisivo combate por defender las conquistas del proceso nacional liberadora; por la eliminación de la dependencia económica y el atraso heredado del colonialismo. Se hizo patente la denuncia al mundo de qué mientras existiera una pulgada del territorio africano en poder extranjero, África no se sentiría verdaderamente libre.

Cabe señalar que 21 años después de su creación, la OUA se ha fortalecido aún más logrando cada vez más éxitos como así lo reiteran los 51 Estados independientes que la constituyen, reforzando aún más el movimiento de los países no alineados y balanceando la correlación de fuerzas en el ámbito internacional a favor del proceso revolucionario mundial; qué tiene a su cabeza ese sistema socialista mundial en la lucha por la paz y el progreso social.

África se ha venido uniendo su voz reclamante a los otros países del tercer mundo en el llamado orden económico internacional que acabara con las relaciones económicas desiguales existentes entre los países capitalistas desarrollados y nuestros países así abriéndonos paso hacia la independencia económica y el desarrollo social.

Es lamentable la condición actual en que se encuentra nuestro continente más querido como consecuencia de la sequía que nos viene azotando desde hace varios años como resultado de la contaminación del medio ambiente. A esta situación se le puede agregar la política injerencista del Fondo Monetario Internacional (FMI) de imponernos condiciones económicas que al fin y al cabo conducen al saqueo de nuestros recursos naturales, por las corporaciones transnacionales, entorpecen nuestro progreso social, dando lugar a una situación triste: "La deuda externa" que es impagable. Ante esta situación la OUA se empeña cada vez aún más en fortalecer la cooperación económica entre los países del continente.

Sin embargo, el imperialismo pretende resignarse en el intento de impedir y convertir al África en una zona de sus intereses vitales y mantenerla en la economía capitalista mundial con el objetivo de resolver por cuenta de ella, las crisis estructurales del capitalismo.

El apoyo sostenido del actual gobierno de Ronald Reagan al régimen de Marruecos en la guerra injusta contra el pueblo saharaui no intimidara nunca al África combatiente para que busque una solución pacífica en el marco de las resoluciones de OUA y no quebrantará jamás la voluntad de su pueblo de combatir hasta lograr la independencia nacional y la paz.

Es preocupante al mismo tiempo percatarse de que todavía en el continente sigue habiendo manchas oscuras. El papel de bastión de la reacción en África asignada a Sudáfrica racista en la estrategia global del imperialismo es una amenaza constante contra el desarrollo independiente de los Estados en el continente y es la causa principal de la intransigencia que asume con respecto a la independencia de Namibia. El rumbo agresivo de Pretoria está enfilado contra el

África libre, contra las conquistas logradas en el curso de una dura lucha por nuestros pueblos. África y el mundo progresista rechazan resueltamente el arreglo interno impuesto por los racistas en la Namibia ocupada ilegalmente y llama a los países imperialistas concernientes a qué cesen de oponerse a un proceso lógico; la culminación de la lucha de Liberación Nacional en África. La SWAPO es y seguirá siendo el representante legítimo de los anhelos del pueblo de Namibia y para cualquiera solución verdadera, en el marco de las Naciones Unidas, hay que contar con ella.

El problema del cono surafricano no es la presencia de los internacionalistas cubanos, sino la política de hegemonía qué pretende llevar al cabo el Gobierno de Pretoria qué está involucrado en campañas calculadoras de agresión, desestabilización y genocidio contra todos los pueblos de la zona. El África combatiente consciente del papel qué tiene que jugar, está resueltamente decidido en su apoyo a la lucha del pueblo sudafricano dirigido por su organización de vanguardia el ANC y así no hace esperar una enérgica condena a la represión desatada por los racistas en el asesinato de sus mejores hijos por el simple hecho de querer vivir digna y decorosamente en su propia patria.

Rechazamos la falsa imagen que los medios de difusión occidental quieren proyectar sobre las llamadas reformas del sistema de apartheid en consonancia con la sucia política de la oligarquía estadounidense catalogada involucramiento constructivo.

Estamos convencidos de que la victoria sobre el inhumano sistema de apartheid es inevitable y será el fruto de sacrificio de los mejores hijos de África quienes confiados en la solidaridad internacional han tomado las calles para decir: ¡No! al sistema oprobioso. No cabe la menor duda de que la dominación de los colonizadores y racistas clásicos toca a su fin.

Compañeros, reciban nuestro agradecimiento por honrarnos con su presencia en este acto, muestra del espíritu solidario e internacionalista del pueblo cubano durante todos los años de su construcción de la nueva sociedad.

Patentizamos nuestra solidaridad con todos los pueblos que en el mundo luchan por el progreso social y la paz, en particular el pueblo de Nicaragua.

¡Viva la unidad africana!

¡Viva la solidaridad internacional!

¡Viva la amistad entre Cuba y África!

¡Con fuerza y razón, Patria o Muerte!

¡Venceremos!

English Speech Text in Commemoration of the Twenty-First Anniversary of the Founding of the OAU

Distinguished comrades at the podium,

Comrades honoring us with your presence in this event,

It makes us feel privileged to reunite with you in the homeland of Martí and Fidel to commemorate yet another anniversary of the Organization for African Unity and thus reaffirm the bonds of friendship and brotherhood that unite us. On a day like this in 1963, the great African statesmen gathered in the admired capital of Ethiopia, Addis Ababa, to create the Organization for African Unity (OAU).

This constituted an event of great historical significance in the struggle carried out by the African people against the most criminal and vandal of colonialist oppression and exploitation. It was there that the action program was drawn up with the contributions of all African people in the decisive fight to defend the conquests of the national liberating process; for the elimination of economic dependency and backwardness inherited from colonialism. A denunciation to the world was made clear that as long as there was an inch of African territory in foreign power; Africa would not truly feel free.

It is worth noting that twenty-one years after its creation, the OAU has been further strengthened, achieving more and more successes, as reiterated by the fifty-one independent states that constitute its membership, further reinforcing the movement of non-aligned countries and balancing the correlation of forces at the international level in favor of the world revolutionary process; headed by the world socialist system, in the struggle for peace and social progress.

Africa has been joining its demanding voice to the other third world countries in the so-called international economic order that will end the unequal economic relations existing between the developed Western countries and ours; thus making way for economic independence and social development.

The current condition of our most beloved continent as a consequence of the drought that has plagued us for several years as a result of environmental pollution is unfortunate. To this situation can be added the interventionist policy of the International Monetary Fund (IMF) of imposing economic conditions on us that, after all, lead to the looting of our natural resources by transnational corporations, hindering our social progress and resulting ultimately in external debt that is unsustainable. Faced with this situation, the OAU is increasingly striving to strengthen economic cooperation between the countries of the continent.

However, imperialism tries to resign itself in the attempt to prevent and turn Africa into a zone for its vital interests and keep it in the world capitalist economy with the aim of solving on its "shoulders," the structural crises inherent in capitalism.

The sustained support of the current Ronald Reagan administration to the Moroccan regime in the unjust war against the people of the region will never intimidate fighting Africa into seeking a peaceful solution within the framework of the OAU resolutions and will never break the will of its people from fighting to achieve national independence and peace.

It is worrisome at the same time to realize that there are still dark spots on the continent. The bastion role assigned to racist South Africa in the imperialist global strategy is a constant threat against the independent development of States on the continent and is the main cause of the intransigence it assumes regarding the independence of Namibia. Pretoria's aggressive course is directed against free Africa, against the conquests achieved in the course of a hard struggle of our people. Africa and the progressive world resolutely reject the internal settlement imposed by the racists in illegally occupied Namibia and ı on the imperialist countries concerned to stop opposing a logical process; the culmination of the National Liberation struggle in Africa. SWAPO is and will continue to be the legitimate representative of the wishes of the Namibian people, and for any real solution, within the framework of the United Nations, it must have a seat at the table.

The problem in the Southern African cone is not the presence of the Cuban internationalists, but the policy of hegemony which the Government of Pretoria insists on carrying out, by engaging in calculated campaigns of aggression, destabilization and genocide against all the peoples of the area. Combatant Africa, aware of the role it has to play, is resolutely determined in its support for the struggle of the South African people led by its vanguard organization, the ANC, and thus does not wait for a mere strong condemnation of the repression unleashed by the racists in the murder of its best children based on the simple fact of wanting to live with dignity and decorum in their own country.

We reject the false image that the Western mass media wishes to project on the so-called reforms of the apartheid system in line with the dirty politics of the American oligarchy, labeled constructive involvement.

We are convinced that victory over the inhumane apartheid system is inevitable and will be the result of the sacrifice of Africa's best children who, trusting in international solidarity, have taken to the streets to say: No!-to the disgraceful system. There is no doubt that the domination of the classical colonizers and their racist sympathizers is quickly coming to an end.

Comrades, receive our thanks for honoring us with your presence at this event, which shows the solidarity and international spirit of the Cuban people during all the years in their construction of a new society.

We patent our solidarity with all the people in the world fighting for social progress and peace, in particular the people of Nicaragua.

Long live African unity!

Long live international solidarity!

Long live the friendship between Cuba and Africa!

With dignity and reason, Homeland or Death!

We shall overcome!

About the Author

This is the first publication for Abel Ndambasha, who has a passion for writing in his leisure time. He holds a master's degree in mechanical engineering from Florida International University, Miami and has been associated with the medical device industry for more than twenty-three years in various roles.

His first attempt at writing occurred as early as primary school when a colleague suggested collaborating on a children's storybook, which was ultimately completed but never published. Since then, he had been consumed by the desire to write and publish. Writing his memoir, therefore, seemed like a logical first step to set his passion for writing in motion and to formally introduce himself to the community of readers. His spheres of exploration include politics and religion. He currently resides in Houston, Texas, where he is also actively involved in several professional organizations related to his work of improving patients' lives in the medical device industry.

For any comments he can be reached through email at andambasha57@gmail.com

9 781649 525000